John F. Kennedy and the Media: The First Television President

Joseph P. Berry Jr.

UNIVERSITY PRESS OF AMERICA

Copyright © 1987 by

University Press of America,® Inc.

4720 Boston Way
Lanham, MD 20706

All rights reserved

Printed in the United States of America

Library of Congress Cataloging-in-Publication Data

Berry, Joseph P., 1955-
  John F. Kennedy and the media.

  Bibliography: p.
  1. Kennedy, John F. (John Fitzgerald), 1917-1963.
2. Television in politics—United States—History—
20th century. 3. Communication in politics—United
States—History—20th century. 4. United States—
Politics and government—1961-1963. I. Title.
E842.1.B47   1987   973.922'4   87-15170
ISBN 0-8191-6552-2 (alk. paper)
ISBN 0-8191-6553-0 (pbk. : alk. paper)

All University Press of America books are produced on acid-free
paper which exceeds the minimum standards set by the National
Historical Publication and Records Commission.

To my parents

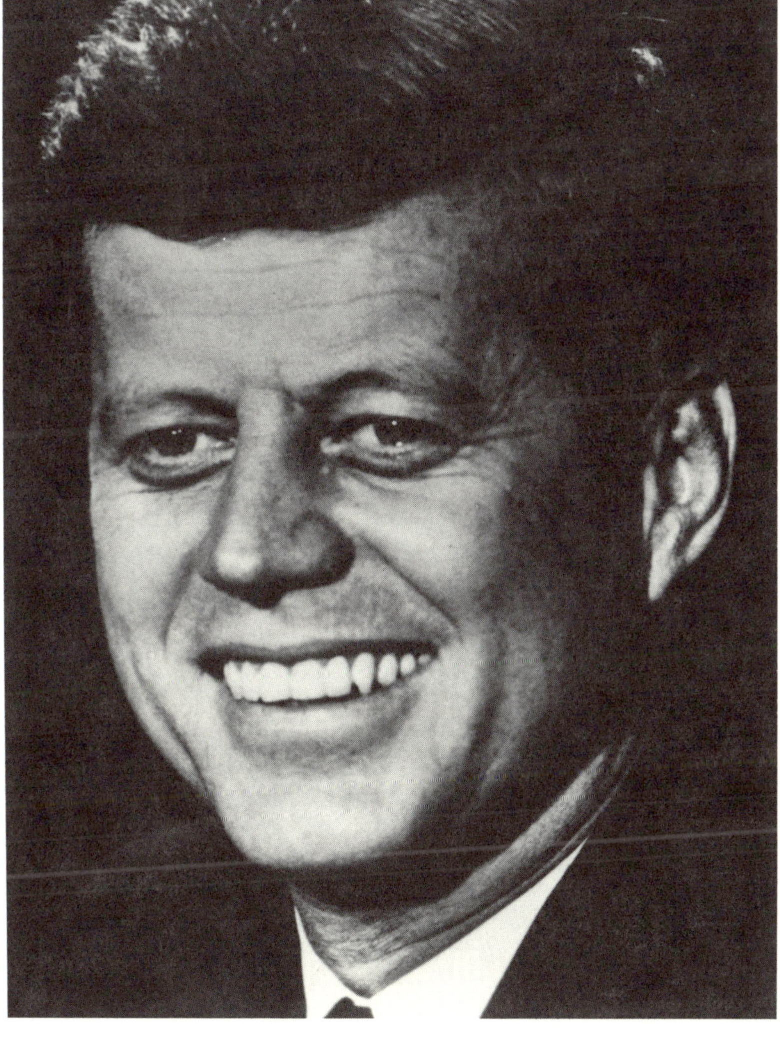

CONTENTS

Prologue 1

1 Tea Parties and Other Media Events 5

2 Kennedy Mesmerizes the Television Audience: A Kaleidoscopic View of Events................................21

3 The Presidential Race 41

4 Kennedy vs. the Media 57

5 Communication Style: A Montage of Images 73

6 Kennedy Humor.......................119

7 The White House Years 137

Epilogue............................147

PROLOGUE

President Kennedy's News Conference of February 21, 1963:

Question: Mr. President, the practice of managed news is attributed to your administration. Mr. Salinger says he has never had it defined. Would you give us your definition, and tell us why you find it necessary to practice it?

The President: You are charging us with something, Mrs. Craig, and then you are asking me to define what it is you are charging me with. I think you might — let me just say we've had very limited success in managing the news, if that's what we have been trying to do. Perhaps you would tell us what it is that you object to in our treatment of the news?

Question: Are you asking me, sir?

The President: Yes.

Question: Well, I don't believe in managed news at all. I thought we ought to get everything we want.

The President: Well, I think that you should, too, Mrs. Craig. I am for that. (Laughter)

All presidents throughout American history, before and after John F. Kennedy, have attempted to manage the news to serve their political interests. Kennedy was the master.

Management of the news was a daily concern of Kennedy's. He was the first president who fully understood and used the media for its political potential. Kennedy once asked Jacqueline Bouvier to postpone their engagement announcement until after the *Saturday Evening Post* printed an article about him, "The Senate's Gay, Young Bachelor." After his assassination, it was revealed that he had prevented the *New York Times* and *New Republic* from reporting the impending CIA sponsored Cuban invasion at the Bay of Pigs during his administration. Not until 1974 did the Kennedy Library disclose Kennedy's handwritten note drafted prior to the invasion, which asked, "Is there a plan to brief and brainwash key press within 12 hours or so?" The note listed the *New York Times*, Walter Lippmann, Marquis Child, and Joseph Alsop, as the ones to be "brainwashed."

Media manipulation was a key factor in the political career of John F. Kennedy. However, "manipulation" should not always be interpreted with negative connotations. Kennedy certainly did not view it that way. Throughout his political career, Kennedy perceived himself as a colleague of the press. After all, his first occupation after his hitch in the Navy was that of journalist. At the age of 29, he served as a special correspondent for International News Service (Hearst) at the founding of the United Nations. Additionally, he became a published author by turning his Harvard senior thesis into a best-selling book, *Why England Slept*. Later, while convalescing from a back operation, he wrote *Profiles In Courage*. Kennedy perceived his "media manipulation" merely as a beneficial exchange of information between two associates. His relationship with *Newsweek's* Benjamin Bradlee, to be discussed in a later chapter, exemplified this notion.

Kennedy probably would never have entered politics had not his brother, Joseph Jr., been killed when his PB4Y Liberator bomber exploded during a World War II secret mission. Joseph P. Kennedy Sr. — Kennedy's father and Franklin Roosevelt's Ambassador to the Court of St. James, England — placed his highest hopes on a political career for young Joe. Joe Jr. once boasted to Harold Laski, his economics professor at the London School of Economics, that he would one day be the first Irish Catholic president of the United States.

After the tragic death of Joe Jr., John, the next oldest son, was looked upon as the one to attain his brother's lofty political goal. Kennedy Sr. encouraged his initially reluctant son to run for a seat in the House of Representatives. When he assumed his brother's political aspirations, it was natural that John Kennedy apply his growing knowledge of the media to his political life since his earliest career interest and experience was in the field of journalism.

Kennedy's communication style also played a salient role in his political successes, and he possessed an uncanny ability to have disagreements with the media and political colleagues without causing permanent rifts. Particularly, his ability to master television was unparalleled in his era.

Throughout this book, JFK's relationship with the media — television and the press — will be examined with an eye toward discovering how he accomplished his political victories.

NOTES

1
"Mr. President": John F. Kennedy, *Public Papers of the Presidents of the United States (1963)* (Washington, D.C.: United States Government Printing Office, 1964), p. 204.
1
Kennedy once asked: Kenneth P. O'Donnell, David F. Powers, and Joe McCarthy, *"Johnny, We Hardly Knew Ye"* (Boston: Little, Brown and Company, 1970), p. 95.

1
After his assassination: Garry Wills, *The Kennedy Imprisonment* (Boston: Little, Brown and Company, 1981), p. 149.

2
"Is there a plan": Ibid.

2
After all: Joan and Clay Blair Jr., *The Search For JFK* (New York: Berkley Publishing Corporation, 1976), p. 371.

2
Joe Jr. once boasted: Peter Collier and David Horowitz, *The Kennedys — An American Drama* (New York: Summit Books, 1984), p. 89.

3
Kennedy Sr. encouraged: Richard J. Whalen, *The Founding Father — The Story of Joseph P. Kennedy* (New York: The New American Library of World Literature, Inc., 1964), p. 392.

1

Tea Parties and Other Media Events

"The New Generation offers a leader — John F. Kennedy."

— Henry Luce, publisher of *Time* and *Life* magazines

1946 Congressional Campaign

When Kennedy first decided to run as a candidate for Boston's Eleventh Congressional District in 1946, he had no strong political base and no firm grasp on how to sway the media. Initially, he relied on the "printed word" media and speeches to local groups. Kennedy did not command the powers that the media wielded until later in his career.

The media can be divided into two separate categories. The traditional "printed word" media are newspapers and magazines, while television and radio represent the "electronic" media. The key advantage which the electronic media have over the print media is in the speed of the delivery of messages. Tony Schwartz, in *Media: The Second God*, noted that the "electronic media have taken over the major portion of the work involved in political campaigning: the printing of leaflets, posters, and brochures, and their distribution by mail or hand."

As examples of the electronic media available to politicians, Schwartz cited televised commercials, debates, discussion shows, and conference phone calls to groups of constituents. Discussion shows, such as CBS's "Face the Nation," provide a format wherein politicians, just by appearing in one studio, may be seen by millions of TV viewers. In 1946, however, the full use of the electronic media would not be realized for many years.

The Kennedy political machine was not as well organized in the beginning as one might have assumed. For instance, the very day when Kennedy was officially to announce his congressional candidacy to the newspapers and radio, he suddenly realized that he had no written speech or news release. To handle this problem, a friend of Ambassador Joseph Kennedy, Boston advertising agency president John Dowd, was enlisted into service. Dowd asked and received assistance from his new public relations director, John

Galvin. Knowing little about the candidate, Galvin wrote the news release after Kennedy arrived at the agency to give his biographical background. A friend of Galvin's, political speech writer Mark Dalton, was called in to draft the radio speech. With speech in hand, Kennedy delivered the first radio talk of his career at WNAC and announced his candidacy for the Eleventh District's Congressional seat.

Admiring the work they had done at a moment's notice, Kennedy hired both Galvin and Dalton. He utilized the services of Galvin's advertising agency for the 1946 race and for the senate races of 1952 and 1958. Mark Dalton, a Harvard Law School graduate, had previously worked as a speech writer for the then Massachusetts Governor Paul Dever. Adept at handling issues and strategy, Dalton was appointed campaign manager. One of Kennedy's friends remarked, "For the next six years, while Jack was in the House of Representatives, he listened more to Mark than anyone else." Having access to an advertising agency and a top speech writer, the Kennedy machine was now on the move.

Kennedy's assets in the 1946 congressional race were the following: name recognition (both his grandfathers were active in local politics); war hero status (led his crew to safety after his PT-109 ship was destroyed); a best-selling book *(Why England Slept)*; a committed family; and money. Also, Joseph Kennedy Sr.'s friendship with Henry Luce, publisher of *Time* and *Life* magazines, led to Luce's composing a stirring introduction of *Why England Slept*. "If John Kennedy is characteristic of the younger generation, and I believe he is," wrote Luce, "many of us would be happy to have the destinies of the Republic turned over to his generation at once." From the introduction came Kennedy's campaign slogan, "The New Generation Offers a Leader — John F. Kennedy."

After Kennedy's PT-109 experience, author John Hershey wrote a flattering report of the incident in the *New Yorker*, which was subsequently reprinted in the *Reader's Digest*. Early in 1945, Kennedy told Paul "Red" Fay, a PT-109 crewman, of his reluctance to use his war hero status in his upcoming campaign. He claimed no desire to "parlay a lost PT boat and a bad back into a political advantage."

However, prior to election day, the ambassador stopped by the Charlestown political headquarters, managed by Dave Powers, a staunch Kennedy political aide, to see how the congressional campaign was going. Upon arrival, he found it buzzing with volunteers making phone calls and mailing *Reader's Digest* reprints about John's PT-109 heroism to every veteran on the voting list. The ambassador remarked to Powers, "I won't worry about Charlestown any more."

Throughout Kennedy's political career, many people suspected that the campaigns were being run by his father. This was true to an extent at first, but as John matured and gained more experience, he gradually assumed control of his political affairs. The ambassador at this time shunned public appearances, fearing that ". . . his reputation as a prewar isolationist and his falling out with the New Deal might . . ." create political damage for his son. The ambassador's role for all future campaigns was then established: observe from the background; make key political and media contacts and recommendations when necessary; send in cash where needed. In the 1960 campaign against Nixon, Kennedy Sr.'s disappearance from the public was so absolute that Republican editorial writers drafted a poem about it, "Jack and Bob will run the show, While Ted's in charge of hiding Joe."

A strict reliance on polls characterized all Kennedy campaigns. In 1946, the ambassador hired the *New York*

Daily News to conduct a private poll of the district. To his relief, it predicted that the candidate would receive as many votes as his nine opponents' combined total.

An innovation that John Kennedy introduced to political campaigning was known as the Kennedy Tea Parties. The model for Tea Parties originated from ambassador and Mrs. Kennedy. While serving in England, they held an annual Fourth of July reception at the American Embassy in London. As an open house to all, the reception provided a relaxed environment for the English to meet the ambassador and his family. It was a superb public relations device.

John Kennedy's Tea Parties were formal receptions — for women only. A reception that he and Dave Powers — later appointed JFK's White House Special Assistant — attended was with a group of Gold Star Mothers at the American Legion Hall in Charlestown. A "Gold Star" was awarded by the government to a mother who lost a son during World War II. At the gathering, Kennedy gave a ten minute speech on the sacrifices of war and his desire for world peace. The excited and impressed mothers surrounded the candidate afterwards to wish him well. Powers commented later, "I don't know what this guy's got. He's no great orator and he doesn't say much, but they certainly go crazy over him." He continued:

> In the evening there would be a rally or a political forum with all the candidates invited, and the house parties. We would arrange with young girls, school teachers or telephone operators or nurses, to invite their friends to a party at their house to meet Jack. The parties would range from small ones, with about fifteen people, to big ones that might take up two or three floors of a three-decker house. A wonderful girl named Ronnie Murphy gave a party at her house at 296 Bunker Hill Street one night where they must have had seventy people. Jack would go to three or four house parties

in a night, one around seven-thirty and the later ones at eight or nine or nine-thirty.

These people who met Jack at the house parties would turn out to be his workers. The next night they would be at our headquarters on Main Street, addressing envelopes or calling people on the telephone.

These initial parties were the precursors to the fine-tuned Kennedy Tea Parties conducted during the 1952 senatorial campaign. They became instrumental in drumming up support for the candidate from women in the community. Since Kennedy sought the endorsements of local newspapers, he used the Tea Parties for much needed publicity.

In the Democratic primary, Kennedy won in a field of ten candidates with 42 percent of the total votes. The November 1946 election proved to be a rout. Kennedy won with 69,000 votes over Republican Lester Bowen who received 26,000 votes. His victories and first experiences with the media were just beginning.

1952 Senatorial Campaign

Kennedy soon became bored with the glamourless life of a congressman. With his boundless ambition, he craved a higher office affording more action and prominence.

In 1952, the incumbents for both the governorship and the senate were running for reelection. Incumbent Democratic Governor Paul Dever wavered between deciding for another run at the governorship or challenging the powerful Republican Senator Henry Cabot Lodge. Finally deciding to run for reelection, Dever opened the door for Kennedy to enter the senate race.

Media manipulation by the Kennedy forces played a key role in Kennedy's victory over Lodge. In this contest, he relied on the public opinion polls, he won two important newspaper endorsements, he donated heavily to Adlai Stevenson's presidential campaign funds to earn his endorsement, and finally he staged Tea Parties to get the votes of Massachusetts' women.

Congressman Kennedy's entrance in the senate race was carefully calculated. Both the congressman and his father believed in the use of public opinion polls as a tool to test political waters. In *The Founding Father*, Richard Whalen described the ambassador's role in the senate campaign:

> In family councils, Joe Kennedy advised his son to take on Lodge, saying, "When you've beaten him, you've beaten the best. Why try for something less?" That confident remark would be widely quoted as typical of the Kennedy fighting spirit, but it disclosed only part of the truth about how Kennedy fought. He never committed himself and his resources to a quixotic battle. He fought to win, but only after being convinced there was a chance of winning. For a year and a half before the 1952 campaign, a pair of paid, full-time Kennedy advance men toured the state, sounding out opinions, wooing local politicians, lining up likely volunteer workers. In addition to their detailed reports, Kennedy carefully weighed the findings of private polls. "You wonder why we're taking on Lodge," he confided in a friend. "We've taken polls. He'll be easier to beat than Leverett Saltonstall."

Understanding how newspapers crave stories of action and overachievement, John Kennedy sent his thousands of volunteers throughout Massachusetts to gather as many signatures as possible on his nomination papers. State law required only a minimum of 2,500 names; Kennedy forces accumulated 262,324 signatures. The number of nominating signatures was the greatest number ever received by a candidate for elective office in Massachusetts. Dave Powers recalled his glee when he delivered the nomination papers to the State House and discovered that Senator Lodge's son, George, a reporter, was there to write the filing-of-papers story for the *Boston Herald*. The congressman scored a decisive media victory.

To capitalize further on this victory, Powers suggested the mailing of a Kennedy personal thank-you letter to each person who signed the nomination papers. The congressman was reluctant to commit the vast amount of money needed to send the "thank-you's," but a trip to a local pub changed his mind. When Powers and Kennedy were in Charlestown one night, they visited Matty Loftus, a Kennedy supporter in 1946 who owned the tavern. A longshoreman approached Kennedy, shook his hand and showed him the thank-you letter he received from the Kennedy office. He then said, "I've been signing nomination papers for politicians around here for the last twenty years. You're the first son of a bitch who ever wrote me a letter thanking me for it." Later that evening Kennedy told Powers to keep on mailing out thank-you letters.

During the 1952 senate race, Kennedy sought to keep his campaign separate from Governor Paul Dever's, the Democratic incumbent. The congressman desired to portray an image of himself unlike traditonal Democrats to the media and voters. In the primary voting, Kennedy finished well ahead of Dever. While both were running unopposed, Kennedy received 75 percent of the total primary vote and Dever, the renowned Democratic party leader, only accumulated 60 percent.

Kennedy was then given unexpected favorable newspaper coverage because the majority Republican press in Massachusetts emphasized his gain and downplayed Dever's showing. The press did this in order to help Dever's Republican opponent, Christian Herter.

Fearing that Herter might ride the coattails of Republican

candidate Dwight Eisenhower to victory, Dever ordered his troops to join offices with many local Kennedy headquarters to create a Kennedy-Dever campaign. Two days after the primary, Dever sent his aides out to put up pictures of himself at Kennedy offices. Subsequently, Kenneth O'Donnell was telephoned by one of the Kennedy office workers who cried, "They've got a picture of Dever as big as City Hall and they want me to turn our headquarters into a Dever headquarters. It will blow our whole operation." O'Donnell instructed him and others to turn the Dever people away as this occurred across the state.

Intervening in this crisis, Ambassador Kennedy instructed Robert Kennedy, the senatorial campaign manager, to allow the Dever people to join with Jack. Robert was adamant to keep the campaigns separate and the congressman agreed. "Don't give in to them," John Kennedy warned his brother, "but don't get me involved in it. Treat it as an organizational problem." The aggressive Robert decided to visit Dever personally to let him know there would be no joint Kennedy-Dever offices outside of Boston. During Robert's tirade, Dever interrupted him and threw him out of his office. Having seen and heard enough of the Kennedy campaign manager, Dever phoned the ambassador, "I know you're an important man around here and all that, but I'm telling you this and I mean it. Keep that fresh kid of yours out of my sight from here on in."

The Kennedy image strategy paid off in victory as Republican landslide victories swept the nation. While Kennedy won in 1952, Dever lost to Christian Herter in a close race. Kennedy was successful in portraying himself to the public and media as an independent thinker, thereby disassociating himself from that year's losing Democrats.

In order to gain Democratic presidential nominee Adlai Stevenson's support, Ambassador Kennedy contributed a large amount of money to his political campaign. In return for this favor, Stevenson visited Massachusetts and endorsed John Kennedy as "my type of guy." The ambassador believed that Stevenson's endorsement, publicized by the state press, was well worth the investment.

Trying to help his son any way he could, the elder Kennedy sought newspaper endorsements during the senate campaign. This would be difficult in a state full of Republican controlled newspapers, but no challenge was too great for the ambassador. Noticing that *New Bedford Standard Times* had a falling-out with Senator Lodge (it denounced him as "a Truman socialist New Dealer"), the elder Kennedy made his move. After the ambassador visited the paper's publisher, Basil Brewer, the *Standard Times* came out with a resounding endorsement of young Kennedy. To an outsider it might appear curious that the conservative Brewer would endorse a liberal Democrat. It appeared that Brewer presumed the conservative ambassador would control his son's liberal ways.

Prior to the election *Boston Post* publisher John Fox had planned to endorse Senator Lodge. Curiously, three weeks before the election, Basil Brewer contacted Fox and asked him to not support Lodge. The then-wavering Fox decided he would still endorse Lodge if only Republican Senators Robert Taft or Joe McCarthy would ask. Since the request was not forthcoming, the *Boston Post* prepared a front page editorial endorsing Kennedy for senator. Fox unsuccessfully attempted to contact Jack Kennedy to inform him of the *Post's* impending endorsement; he then requested and received a meeting with the ambassador. At the meeting, the elder Kennedy was overcome with elation at hearing about the paper's forthcoming endorsement. "He told me then," Fox recalled, "that if I needed anything in the world, all I had to do was ask him." Fox then informed him of the paper's financial difficulties and the ambassador soon thereafter issued a $500,000 loan. Years later, Fox denied the endorsement was exchanged for the loan. However, John Kennedy later commented to a Harvard classmate, Fletcher Knebel, about the *Boston Post* endorsement: "You know we had to buy that fucking paper, or I'd have been licked."

What most impressed political professionals was the extreme attention to details paid by the Kennedy machine during the senate campaign. Whalen further discussed the Kennedy's control of information:

> The magnitude of the Kennedy publicity was staggering. Distributed across the state were nine hundred thousand copies of an eight-page tabloid featuring drawings of Lieutenant Kennedy rescuing his shipmates in the Pacific. On the facing page was a photograph of young Joe Kennedy, whose fatal war mission was described under this headline: "John Fulfills Dream of Brother Joe Who Met Death in the Sky Over the English Channel." Inserted in each paper was a *Reader's Digest* reprint of John Hersey's article on the saga of PT-109, which originally appeared in the *New Yorker*.
>
> Still, the most impressive feature in this vast campaign — indeed, the Kennedy hallmark — was painstaking attention to small details. In June, Boston's Mayor John B. Hynes appeared at a rally at the Copley-Plaza launching Jack Kennedy's campaign. "The speeches were televised," Hynes later recalled, "and for the first time I saw a teleprompter. In fact, there were *two* of them, and I wondered why." When one broke down and the other kept the show running smoothly, Hynes realized he was in the company of perfectionists.

Once again, the most publicized and successful media events staged during the campaign were the Kennedy Tea Parties. Originated by the family for the congressional race, they were perfected in the senatorial campaign.

Kennedy aides mailed engraved invitations to every woman on a particular community's voting list. The invitation asked the woman to come and meet the candidate and his family members. The attraction of meeting Rose Kennedy, the famous wife of the former ambassador to England, caught the interest of the locality. Additionally, young women were excited at the prospect of meeting bachelor John. A precinct worker in Boston commented, "Before the teas, the hairdressers were working overtime and the dressmakers were taking dresses in and letting dresses out. Every girl in the district was dreaming and hoping that maybe lightning would strike."

During the senatorial race, a total of 35 Tea Parties were staged, attracting approximately 75,000 guests, mostly women, and that number was about the same margin by which Kennedy beat Lodge. Despondent about the loss, Lodge was quoted as saying, "It was those damned Tea Parties." In the following years Senator Kennedy was introduced frequently at political functions as "the man who drowned Henry Cabot Lodge in 75,000 cups of tea."

NOTES

7
"electronic media have taken over": Tony Schwartz, *Media: The Second God* (Garden City, New York: Anchor Books, 1983), p. 103.
7
As examples of the electronic media: Ibid.

7
The Kennedy political machine: Kenneth P. O'Donnell, David F. Powers, and Joe McCarthy, *"Johnny, We Hardly Knew Ye"* (Boston: Little, Brown and Company, 1970), pp. 57f.

8
"For the next six years": Ibid., p. 58.

8
"If John Kennedy is characteristic": Ibid., p. 50.

8
"The New Generation": Ibid.

9
After Kennedy's PT-109 experience: Ibid., p. 46.

9
"parlay a lost PT boat": Ibid.

9
Throughout Kennedy's political career: Richard J. Whalen, *The Founding Father — The Story of Joseph P. Kennedy* (New York: The New American Library of World Literature, Inc., 1964), p. 422.

9
"I won't worry": O'Donnell, Powers, and McCarthy, p. 66.

9
"his reputation as a prewar isolationist": Ibid., p. 65.

9
"Jack and Bob will run the show": Whalen, p. 456.

9
A strict reliance on polls: Ibid., p. 399.

10
The model for Tea Parties: Rose Kennedy, *Times To Remember* (Garden City, New York: Doubleday & Company, Inc., 1974), p. 319.

10
A reception that he: See O'Donnell, Powers, and McCarthy, p. 54.

10
"I don't know what this guy's got": Ibid.
10
"In the evening": Ibid., p. 64.
11
In the Democratic primary: Ibid., p. 71.
11
Kennedy won: Ibid.
11
In 1952, the incumbents: Ibid., pp. 77ff.
12
"In family councils": Whalen, p. 419.
12
Understanding how newspapers crave stories: See O'Donnell, Powers, and McCarthy, pp. 90f.
13
"I've been signing nomination papers": Ibid., p. 91.
13
During the 1952 senate race: Ibid., pp. 87ff.
14
"They've got a picture of Dever": Ibid., p. 88.
14
"Don't give in to them": Ibid.
14
"I know you're an important man": Whalen, p. 421.
14
In order to gain: Ibid., p. 425.
15
"my type of guy": Ibid.
15
Trying to help his son: Ibid.
15
"a Truman socialist New Dealer": Ibid.
15
Prior to the election: Ibid., pp. 429ff.

15
"He told me then": Ibid., p. 431.
16
"You know we had to buy": Ralph G. Martin, *A Hero For Our Time —An Intimate Story of the Kennedy Years* (New York: Macmillan Publishing Company, 1983), p. 58.
16
"The magnitude of the Kennedy publicity": Whalen, p. 423.
17
Kennedy aides mailed engraved invitations: See O'Donnell, Powers, and McCarthy, p. 64f.
17
"Before the teas": Ibid., p. 65.
17
During the senatorial race: Ibid., p. 89.
17
"It was those damned Tea Parties": Whalen, p. 433.
17
"the man who drowned Henry Cabot Lodge": O'Donnell, Powers, and McCarthy, p. 89.

2

Kennedy Mesmerizes the Television Audience: A Kaleidoscopic View of Events

". . . Over and over again there was the handsome, open-faced candidate on the TV screen, showing himself, proving that a Catholic wears no horns."

— Theodore White

While some people feared the advent of television coverage at presidential press conferences, Kennedy welcomed it. James Reston, the columnist, once said that Kennedy's proposal for the live transmission of these events was "the goofiest idea since the hula hoop."

At the January 25, 1961 press conference, a reporter expressed apprehension about its instantaneous transmission, fearing that inadvertent statements, as made in days prior to TV broadcasts, would no longer be correctible. Kennedy explained his feelings on this subject:

> Well, it was my understanding that the statements made... by President Eisenhower were on the record. There may have been a clarification that could have been issued afterwards, but... it still would have been on the record as a clarification, so that I don't think that the interests of our country are — it seems to me they're as well protected under this system as they were under the system followed by President Eisenhower. And this system has the advantage of providing more direct communication.

Kennedy's fascination with the electronic media did not end with national television broadcasts. His July 23, 1962 press conference was transmitted for the first time internationally by the Telstar satellite. He perceived satellite communication as an instrument for peace. "I understand that part of today's press conference is being relayed by the Telstar communications satellite to viewers across the Atlantic, and this is another indication of the extraordinary world in which we live," Kennedy said in his opening remarks. "This satellite must be high enough to carry messages from both sides of the world, which is, of course, a very essential requirement for peace; and I think this understanding which will inevitably come from the speedier communications is bound to increase the well-being and security of all people here and across the oceans."

Kennedy thrived on using television to further his political ambition. As the following discussion will show, Kennedy truly mesmerized his television audiences.

Image Control

The senate swearing-in ceremony was set for January 3, 1953. On that day Kennedy's new personal secretary, Evelyn Lincoln, along with other members of the staff, were preparing to leave the office to attend the ceremony.

"Where is his blue shirt?" a Kennedy aide asked Mrs. Lincoln.

"Why does he want a blue shirt?" she wondered.

"In case he might be on television," came the reply.

As early as 1953, Kennedy had an astute understanding of the impact of television. From his first day in office as senator, Kennedy sought to project his attractive appearance over television, the newest electronic medium. TV was good to Kennedy; during his political career he appeared on it as often as possible. When he was busy making speeches during the 1952 senate race, Kennedy's sisters, Eunice, Pat, and Jean, were in another part of Massachusetts campaigning and showing audiences a film of a flattering interview he gave on the TV show "Meet the Press."

On November 22, 1963, Kennedy took a short thirteen minute trip from Carswell Air Force Base in Forth Worth to Love Field in Dallas by plane rather than by car so that he and his wife could receive an enthusiastic welcome from an awaiting airport crowd. Airport welcomes provide a dramatic scenario for television to record, and the Dallas trip was planned as just another stop for the incumbent president's 1964 reelection campaign.

Image-conscious Kennedy would be quick to cancel any prerecorded films which showed him in an unfavorable light.

At the beginning of JFK's administration, Attorney General Robert Kennedy was eager to portray himself as a champion of civil rights. Without the president's knowledge, Robert had instructed his press relations office in the Justice Department to grant permission for a television network to record a White House meeting scheduled between him and the president. The purpose of the meeting was for Robert to convince his brother to initiate immediate action on a proposed civil rights bill. For political reasons, the president planned to introduce a new tax reduction bill prior to the civil rights bill. The resulting film showed a visably uncomfortable president debating with the attorney general and his Justice Department assistants over civil rights. Fearing the worst, the president asked Kenneth O'Donnell's opinion of the appearance, "You looked like a frightened antelope." The network was persuaded to cancel all showings of the film.

David Halberstam, in *The Best and the Brightest*, wrote that while TV helped Kennedy into the executive branch of government, its effect actually hurt his image during his first year in office. Kennedy had promised to get the country moving again but did not mention that he would have to struggle against a lethargic congress. Halberstam explained further:

> He [Kennedy] was the first of a new kind of media candidate flashed daily into our consciousness during the campaign, and as such he had managed to stir the aspirations and excited millions of people. It had all been deliberately done; he had understood television and used it well, knowing that it was his medium, but it was done at a price. Millions of people watching this driving, handsome young man believed that he could change things, move things, and that their personal problems would somehow be different, lighter, easier with his election. As president, Kennedy was faced with

that great gap of any modern politician, but perhaps greatest in contemporary America: the gap between the new unbelievable velocity of modern life which can send information and images hurtling through the air onto the television screen, exciting desires and appetites, changing mores almost overnight, and the slowness of traditional governmental institutions produced by ideas and laws of another era, bound in normal bureaucratic red tape and traditional seniority.

To compensate for this time lag of putting ideas into action, Kennedy would seek to control his image in other ways, such as the film portrayal of his PT-109 experience. As mentioned in Chapter One, John Hersey's account of the PT-109 story was used as a campaign handout during both the congressional and senate races. In both cases, the article aided Kennedy's political victories. Fortunately for Kennedy's planned reelection campaign for 1964, Hollywood decided to make a movie, entitled *PT-109*, depicting his heroism during World War II. The film was based on a best-selling book written by Robert Donovan. While in office, Kennedy approved the script and director. When his first choice for the star, Warren Beatty, declined the role, he then chose Cliff Robertson who accepted.

In contrast to Kennedy's control over the making of *PT-109*, Ohio Senator John Glenn, 1984 presidential candidate, insisted publically that he had had no controlling influence over the production of the movie *The Right Stuff*. This movie was adapted from Tom Wolfe's book by the same name. It told of America's first attempts at manned space travel during NASA's Mercury program. Glenn, the first American to orbit the Earth in space, had his role in the Mercury program portrayed favorably in the film. The flattering media coverage that Glenn received because of the movie was analogous to how the *PT-109* film might have helped Kennedy in his 1964 reelection campaign.

In both instances, the movies enhanced their heroic images. A key difference, however, was that while Kennedy dominated unblushingly the production of *PT-109*, Glenn purposefully kept his distance from the making of *The Right Stuff* to obviate charges of manipulation.

Kennedy used television to overcome three major obstacles to his being elected president: to become a nationally recognizable political figure; to prove a Catholic could be elected by discussing this issue openly; to show that despite his youth, he was not "too inexperienced."

Kennedy's appearance at the 1956 Democratic National Convention in Chicago, more than anything else, delivered him into national prominence. The great response he received after giving three spectacular televised speeches convinced him that he had a realistic chance at the presidency.

Entering the 1960 primaries and discussing openly his religion on television was the only way Kennedy envisioned a Catholic could win. By winning the West Virginia primary — a state which had a 95 percent Protestant population — he began to soften the voices of the people who thought he was just another Al Smith (Catholic presidential candidate defeated overwhelmingly in 1928). His TV battle with Hubert Humphrey proved to be instrumental in that victory.

In order to overcome the claim that he was "too inexperienced" to be president, Kennedy participated in the 1960 televised debates with Nixon. During the debates, Kennedy appeared as knowledgeable as Nixon on all major issues, foreign and domestic. The remainder of this chapter should help to demonstrate how Kennedy employed the television medium to win the right to reside at 1600 Pennsylvania Avenue.

1956 Democratic National Convention

Three televised events at the 1956 Democratic National Convention fueled the presidential ambitions of Senator Kennedy. The events that brought Kennedy national attention were his narration of *The Pursuit of Happiness*, his nomination speech for Adlai Stevenson, and his vice presidential concession speech.

The Chicago convention began on August 15, 1956. On that night, Kennedy narrated a pre-recorded film, *The Pursuit of Happiness*, which documented the history of the Democratic Party. At the conclusion of the well received film, the senator was introduced to the delegates' warm applause. Kennedy banners, buttons, and volunteers arose from the New England and Chicago sections. Delegates began discussing the possibility of the Massachusetts senator as the vice presidential nominee.

Just as pleasing to Senator Kennedy as the delegates' reaction was the national televising of the film by all TV networks. CBS-TV producers, however, thought that the film was too long for its viewers so it showed only a part of it and then covered other events at the convention. CBS reporter Charles Collingwood, a neighbor and friend of Kennedy's from Georgetown, later joked to the senator, "Well, you didn't make CBS." A visibly angered Kennedy steamed, "I know, you bastards." Afterwards Collingwood said, "I was shocked into silence. I just didn't know it meant that much to him."

Kennedy's hopes of being nominated vice president faded when presidential nominee, Adlai Stevenson, asked him to give his nomination speech. At that time, nominating speeches were delivered traditionally by the leading runner-up for vice presidential nominee. Seizing this opportunity with "vigah" (one of Kennedy's favorite words), he reviewed the drafted nominating speech given to him by the Stevenson staff. Kennedy dismissed summarily the Stevenson draft, which his speech writer Sorensen described as a "wordy, corny, lackluster committee product."

Standing near the podium with his rewritten version of the speech, Kennedy prepared to address the delegates and national television audience. Tom Winship, a reporter with the *Boston Globe*, was on the scene and saw the senator's intensity as he walked to the podium. "I remember the way he clenched his fists," the reporter said, "and whispered to himself, 'Go!' Then he pushed himself towards the podium and gave his speech."

In the address, the senator labeled Eisenhower and Nixon as "one who took the high road and one who took the low." This phrase was picked up and used repeatedly in speeches by other Democrats during that campaign year. Kennedy excited the nation with his words and delivery:

> We here today are selecting a man who must be more than a good politician, or a good liberal, or a good conservative. We are selecting the head of the most powerful nation on earth — the man who literally will hold in his hands the power of survival or destruction, of freedom or slavery... We have, therefore, an obligation to pick the best man qualified, not only to lead our party, but to lead our country. The nation is entitled to expect that of us... What we do here today affects more than a nomination, more than an election — it affects the life and way of life of all our fellow Americans. The time is ripe. The hour has struck. The man is here; and he is ready. Let the word go forth that we have fulfilled our responsibility to the nation.

Having won and accepted the Democratic presidential nomination, Stevenson — to the surprise of all — broke tradition and opened the convention so that the delegates could choose the vice presidential nominee. Kennedy's staff mounted a frantic effort at winning the nomination. After falling short in votes to Estes Kefauver, the senator had another chance to address the nation on television. Turning adversity into opportunity, Kennedy, without notes, gave the concession speech and asked the convention to make Kefauver's nomination unanimous. James MacGregor Burns described the scene:

> He appeared as calm in defeat as in the prospect of victory. At the Convention Hall, he pushed his way to the rostrum: "Ladies and gentlemen of this convention. I want to take this opportunity to express my appreciation to Democrats from all parts of the country...." Despite his grin, Kennedy looked wilted and disappointed. Yet as things turned out, this was his greatest moment — the moment when he passed through a kind of political sound barrier to register on the nation's memory. The dramatic race had glued millions to their television sets. Kennedy's near victory and sudden loss — the impression of a clean-cut boy who had done his best and who was accepting defeat with a smile — all this struck at people's hearts in living rooms across the nation. In this moment in triumphant defeat, his campaign for the presidency was born.

Capitalizing on the energy, enthusiasm, and popularity of his Stevenson nominating speech and vice presidential concession speech, Kennedy had films of the speeches shown throughout Massachusetts during his victorious 1958 senate reelection campaign. Kennedy's aide, Mike Feldman, believed that their greatest political asset that year was the concession speech film. "It was almost the centerpiece of our campaign publicity," said Feldman, "because it always attracted crowds. Always."

West Virginia Primary

A classic TV battle during the 1960 campaign for president was waged between Kennedy and Hubert Humphrey in the

West Virginia primary. The wealthy Kennedys aired well-orchestrated, professionally prepared TV promotions, while the financially strapped Humphrey campaign used rambling and disorganized methods such as TV telethons. Humphrey's total expenditures in West Virginia came to $25,000, while the Kennedy team spent $34,000 on television alone.

The real test for Kennedy in West Virginia was to determine whether a Catholic could win in a 95 percent Protestant state. Having the battle lines drawn clearly, Kennedy deftly prepared to use TV to achieve victory. Cognizant that pollster Lou Harris in December 1959 found him with a 70 to 30 percent advantage over Humphrey, Kennedy decided to enter the West Virginia contest. Shortly after he entered, however, a second Harris poll taken after his primary victory in Wisconsin, brought the religious issue to full light; it revealed a 60 to 40 percent margin for Humphrey. Now, more than ever, Kennedy needed to utilize TV to the best of his ability.

Theodore White described one slick TV documentary film Kennedy aired to overcome the religious issue:

> ... over and over again there was the handsome, open-faced candidate on the TV screen, showing himself, proving that a Catholic wears no horns. The documentary film on TV opened with a cut of a PT boat spraying a white wake through the black night, and Kennedy was a war hero; the film next showed the quiet young man holding a book in his hand in his own library receiving a Pulitzer Prize, and he was a scholar; then the young man held his golden-curled daughter of two, reading to her as she sat on his lap, and he was a young father; and always, gravely, open-eyed, with a sincerity that could not be feigned, he would explain his own devotion to the freedom of America's faiths and the separation of church and state.

JOHN F. KENNEDY AND THE MEDIA: THE FIRST TELEVISION PRESIDENT

In contrast to the professional Kennedy TV campaign, Humphrey ran a haphazard TV telethon. Telethons are a political gimmick in which a candidate theoretically accepts any and all phone calls from members of a TV viewing audience who contact the local station. Effective telethons have a candidate's staff screen callers to organize questions in a fashion that allows the candidate to discuss the issues which best relate to his campaign.

Due to a lack of preparation and money, Humphrey conducted an actual TV telethon by accepting all unscreened calls from the public in the order that they came in. The result? Total disaster. After fielding some initially easy questions, e.g., "What makes you think you're qualified to be president, Senator Humphrey?", he then received a call from an elderly woman who yelled, "You git out of West Virginia, Mr. Humphrey!" and berated him for challenging the Republican leadership in the country. Subsequent calls resulted in a series of rambling, disjointed discussions which did not allow Humphrey to outline his campaign program. After watching Humphrey's performance, Theodore White observed, ". . . TV is no medium for a poor man."

Trying to reestablish his lead, Humphrey challenged Kennedy to debate on television. Since both of their positions on the campaign issues were similar, there were no salient debating points to argue. However, during the debate, Kennedy demonstrated his cool, rational demeanor — ideal for television — and also appealed to the viewers' emotions by displaying the meager contents of a government food-ration package of which many unemployed West Virginia families had to subsist on. By using these "props" on TV, he showed more concern than Humphrey about the plight of the state's poor. Local newspapers reported voters switching their allegiance from Humphrey to Kennedy soon after the debate.

Kennedy closed the primary campaign on a well-planned, televised question-and-answer show with Franklin D. Roosevelt Jr., who was popular in West Virginia because of his father. Theodore Sorensen wrote the toughest questions which he could think of on the religious issue for Roosevelt to ask. In West Virginia, the strategy was to attack the issue head-on and let the voters decide who was the best candidate. In order to allay the Protestants' fears about his Catholic religion, Kennedy promised during the TV show that as president he "would not take orders from any Pope, Cardinal, Bishop, or priest . . . ." The well-organized TV show undoubtedly contributed to Kennedy's surprising victory margin over Humphrey, 61 to 39 percent.

Houston Minister's Speech

Thinking mistakenly that West Virginia put the religious issue behind him, Kennedy was later invited to discuss his Catholic religion before the Greater Houston Ministerial Association in Houston, Texas on September 12, 1960. Choosing action over inaction, he accepted the challenge.

While writing the text of the speech, Kennedy worked with Theodore Sorensen (a Unitarian) at the Ambassador Hotel in Los Angeles. The weekend prior to the speech, Sorensen confided his feelings to a friend, "We can win or lose the election right there in Houston on Monday night."

The agreed upon format called for Kennedy to respond to the ministers' questions, after giving his prepared speech. Facing an audience of approximately 600 people, evenly divided between ministers and spectators, and with TV cameras rolling, he once again attempted to alleviate the nation's fears of electing a Catholic president:

> . . . I believe in an America where the separation of Church and State is absolute — where no Catholic prelate would tell

the president (should he be a Catholic) how to act, and no Protestant minister would tell his parishioners for whom to vote — where no church or church school is granted any public funds or political preference — and where no man is denied public office merely because his religion differs from the president who might appoint him or the people who might elect him . . .

. . . That is the kind of America in which I believe. And it represents the kind of presidency in which I believe — a great office that must be neither humbled by making it the instrument of any religious group, nor tarnished by arbitrarily withholding its occupancy from the members of any religious group. I believe in a president whose views on religion are his own private affairs, neither imposed upon him by the nation or imposed upon him as a condition to holding that office . . . .

His speech and responses to questions were well-received and he won the applause from the initially skeptical audience. Segments of the film taken in Houston were shown the next day on national TV networks throughout the country. Thus once again, the electronic medium transmitted a speech, given only to hundreds, magnified to an audience of millions. The responses to the speech were so favorable that Kennedy volunteers showed the Houston film to various audiences across the nation for the duration of the presidential campaign.

The Great Debates

The 1960 Kennedy-Nixon Debates crystalized to a battle of appearances and images. Also, Kennedy, the lesser known candidate, gained prominence by receiving prime time TV coverage with Vice-President Richard Nixon.

Of all the post debate surveys conducted, not one can definitively name the winner of each of the four debates. However, the general consensus of opinion was that

Kennedy Mesmerizes the Television Audience

Kennedy overcame the public's perceived image of him as too immature and too inexperienced to lead the free world. This image reversal may have been crucial in Kennedy's narrow presidential win over Nixon. Kennedy accomplished this victory by demonstrating his broad awareness of all the issues and by quickly citing pertinent facts and statistics to support his statements.

The physical contrast between the candidates was most striking in the first debate. Kennedy looked healthy, tanned and wore a dark blue suit, which contrasted well with the light greyish background. Nixon's grey suit blended into the background, and he looked physically ill due to his recent convalescence from a knee operation. To compensate for his heavy beard, Nixon had an aide plaster his face with a pancake cosmetic, called Max Factor's "Lazy Shave."

Throughout the debates, Kennedy displayed more energy and enthusiasm than Nixon. While a reporter would be asking him a question, Kennedy would sometimes cut him off to fire a response. The nation heard Kennedy's distinctive Boston accent showcased in this format, which had helped to differentiate him from other candidates previously on the campaign trail. Reaction shots of Kennedy showed him looking directly at Nixon, concentrating on what he was saying. Nixon, during reaction shots, would sometimes gaze uncomfortably at the camera. Nixon was also caught once showing nervousness by wiping sweat from his face with a handkerchief.

Both Kennedy and Nixon sought to manipulate the format and setting of the debates. Prior to one debate Kennedy complained that there were more spotlights on him than on Nixon and he proceeded to rearrange them. Nixon insisted on keeping the studio air conditioning as low as tolerable to eliminate his facial perspiration, while Kennedy complained that he might have to start wearing a sweater underneath his coat. Kennedy pressed for more reaction shots during the debates because he felt that they benefited him more than Nixon.

Nixon's participation in the debates was dependent on an understanding which he stipulated in his acceptance letter to the networks: "In general, it is my position that joint television appearances of the presidential candidates should be conducted as full and free exchange of views without prepared texts or notes, and without interruption...." Nixon later accused Kennedy of disregarding the agreed upon format because, in the third debate, Kennedy read from two printed quotations and from a photocopy of an Eisenhower letter. Kennedy aides denied that there was any rule prohibiting the use of notes.

At the conclusion of the four TV debates, Kennedy felt confident that this medium showed him at his best. Through a letter, he urged Nixon to meet with him for a fifth or possibly even additional debates. At the time, the Nixon camp did consider another debate, but time was short since election day was fast approaching. In the rush to set up a fifth debate, neither side could agree on the format and, due to the resulting confusion, it never transpired.

In Marshall McLuhan's terms, John Kennedy can be perceived as a cool candidate on a cool medium: television. Knowing the effect of TV on politicking, he took full advantage of it. Campaigning for president, Kennedy demonstrated a futuristic understanding of television. "The timing of his half-hour shows was carefully selected with an eye to what programs would be displaced, thus displeasing their fans," Sorensen revealed. "Five minute 'spot' presentations were also strategically placed at the end of popular shows." Ready for any format, Kennedy prepared "single issue" film presentations to be shown where and when deemed appropriate. Remarkably, Kennedy even thought in terms of what is now called "local color" to serve as the background in his TV live appearances and filmed presentations.

Some politicians, however, did not comprehend the importance of television until later in life. "Unfortunately, in the television age a candidate's appearance and style count for more than his ideas and record," lamented Richard Nixon in a 1984 interview. "An intelligent candidate who follows his conscience and runs a campaign based entirely on substance — who worries more about getting his views across than about what color shirt will look best on the evening news — is a sure loser."

NOTES

23
"the goofiest idea": Theodore C. Sorensen, *Kennedy* (New York: Bantam Books, Inc., 1965), p. 361.
23
"Well, it was my understanding": John F. Kennedy, *Public Papers of the Presidents of the United States (1961)* (Washington, D.C.: United States Government Printing Office, 1962), p. 10.
23
"I understand that": John F. Kennedy, *Public Papers of the Presidents of the United States (1962)* (Washington, D.C.: United States Government Printing Office, 1963), p. 568.
24
"Where is his blue shirt?": Evelyn Lincoln, *My Twelve Years With John F. Kennedy* (New York: Bantam Books, Inc., 1965), p. 12.

24
When he was busy making speeches: Rose Kennedy, *Times To Remember* (Garden City, New York: Doubleday & Company, Inc., 1974), p. 323.

24
Airport welcomes: Kenneth P. O'Donnell, David F. Powers, and Joe McCarthy, *"Johnny, We Hardly Knew Ye"* (Boston: Little, Brown and Company, 1970), p. 25.

24
Image-conscious Kennedy: Ibid., pp. 6f.

25
"You looked like a frightened antelope": Ibid., p. 7.

25
"He [Kennedy] was the first": David Halberstam, *The Best and the Brightest* (New York: Random House, 1969), pp. 64f.

26
While in office: Garry Wills, *The Kennedy Imprisonment* (Boston: Little, Brown and Company, 1981), p. 134.

26
In contrast to Kennedy's control: See *Los Angeles Times*, September 22, 1983, p. 14.

27
Entering the 1960 primaries: See Sorensen, pp. 160ff.

28
The Pursuit of Happiness: See Rose Kennedy, pp. 327ff.; Sorensen, pp. 96ff.; and Ralph G. Martin, *A Hero For Our Time — An Intimate Story of the Kennedy Years* (New York: Macmillan Publishing Company, 1983), p. 108.

28
"Well, you didn't make CBS.": Ibid., pp. 108f.

28
Kennedy's hopes of being nominated: See Lincoln, p. 65.

29
"wordy, corny, lackluster committee product": Sorensen, p. 97.
29
"I remember the way": Martin, p. 109.
29
"one who took the high road": Sorensen, p. 97.
29
"We here today": Lincoln, pp. 65f.
30
"He appeared as calm": Rose Kennedy, p. 329.
30
"It was almost the centerpiece": Martin, p. 132.
30
A Classic TV battle: Details of the West Virginia primary are in Theodore H. White, *The Making Of The Presidency 1960* (New York: Atheneum House, Inc., 1961), pp. 116ff.
31
". . . over and over again": Ibid., p. 128.
32
"What makes you think": Ibid., pp. 131f.
32
". . . TV is no medium": Ibid., p. 133.
33
"Would not take orders": Sorensen, p. 164.
33
"We can win": White, p. 296.
33
"I believe in an America": Ibid., p. 297.
34
Segments of the film: Ibid., p. 298.
34
The Great Debates: Details of The Great Debates are in Sidney Kraus (ed.), *The Great Debates — Kennedy vs.*

Nixon, 1960 (Bloomington: Indiana University Press, 1962). Also see Sorensen, pp. 220ff.

35
To compensate for his heavy beard: Kraus, p. 85.

36
"In general, it is my position": Ibid., p. 113.

36
"The timing of his half-hour shows": Sorensen, pp. 220f.

37
"Unfortunately, in the television age": Richard Nixon, "What's Wrong With The Way We Pick Our Presidents," *U.S. News & World Report*, Vol. 97, No. 4, July 23, 1984, p. 30.

3

The Presidential Race

"We're going to sell Jack like soap flakes."

— Joseph Kennedy Sr.

The media attention generated after Kennedy's performance at the 1956 Democratic National Convention encouraged the senator to pursue the presidency. Most of Kennedy's activities between 1956 and 1960 were geared to developing a politically positive media image.

As a result of Kennedy's new found publicity, *Time* magazine wrote its first cover story about him that said, "Jack Kennedy has left panting politicians and swooning women across a large spread of the U.S." During this time, he was the subject of twelve cover stories by different magazines. He also gained more publicity by writing more than three dozen magazine articles.

"We're going to sell Jack like soap flakes," Joseph Kennedy Sr. once told a friend of his while discussing his son's magnetic appeal. During an interview in 1959, Ambassador Kennedy said to a reporter, "I'll tell you how to sell more copies of a 'book.' Put his picture on the cover. Why is it that when his picture is on the cover of *Life* or *Redbook* that they sell a record number of copies?"

John Kennedy, accompanied by aide Ted Sorensen, spent many days after the 1956 convention campaigning on behalf of Adlai Stevenson. His barnstorming throughout the country gave him his first taste of national politicking, and he enjoyed it. It was during this trek that the senator made key political contacts, gained valuable campaigning experience, and drew the attention of the local and national media.

At this time, Mrs. Lincoln, Kennedy's secretary, was overwhelmed with handling the more than 2,500 speaking invitations that he received. It became obvious that Kennedy had impressed the entire nation during the televised 1956 Democratic Convention because the invitations came from all parts of the country. Thinking in terms of public relations, Kennedy asked, "Mrs. Lincoln, why don't you keep a tally on these invitations? If we continue to get them in such large quantities, I am sure the reporters would be interested." The media coverage gained was astounding. Not only did the press periodically check back with the Kennedy office to get the latest count, but columnists in their reports began to analyze the meaning of these figures.

One campaign document that enhanced Kennedy's political aspirations was his book, *Profiles In Courage*. Written with the researching assistance of Theodore Sorensen and others, it described eight American politicians whose careers exemplified political courage. The book established Kennedy's image as an intellectual.

When young John considered publishing his Harvard thesis, *Why England Slept*, his father advised:

> You would be surprised how a book really makes the grade with high-class people stands you in good stead for years to come. I remember that in the report you are asked to make after twenty-five years to the committee at Harvard, one of the questions is "What books have you written?" and there is no doubt you will have done yourself a great deal of good.

Further media coverage blanketed Kennedy when he won a Pulitzer Prize for *Profiles In Courage*. Did he win the award strictly on the merits of the book? Garry Wills, in *The Kennedy Imprisonment*, reported that Ambassador Kennedy's friend, *New York Times* correspondent Arthur Krock, lobbied on behalf of the Kennedys for the Pulitzer Prize. Due to the book's national appeal, Kennedy was selected chairman for a special senate committee. Its mission was to select the five most outstanding senators in the history of the United States for official recognition.

1958 Senatorial Campaign

The next step needed in Kennedy's quest for the White House meant winning his 1958 senate reelection. He decided that in order to impress powerful politicians throughout the nation of his ability to get votes, he would press for the largest victory margin possible. As mentioned in the previous chapter, the senator used television extensively in this campaign, particularly the films of his speeches given at the 1956 convention.

In Massachusetts were two small Republican communities, Washington and Mashpee, in which the residents traditionally voted early in the morning on election day. They did this in order to have their voting results reported as front page stories in the early afternoon Massachusetts' newspapers thereby giving the impression that the Republican candidates had a strong lead in the voting. Realizing this practice, a determined Edward "Ted" Kennedy attempted to persuade the two Republican communities to switch their votes that year to John Kennedy in the 1958 race. Ted visited the homes of the residents in this effort. Surprisingly, the newspapers printed on election day showed Kennedy leading in both towns by a margin of 181 to 90. The youngest Kennedy brother was learning how to manipulate the media.

John Kennedy realized his goal by winning his reelection by the largest margin won by any senatorial candidate in the nation that year. In contrast to the 1952 campaign, not one Massachusetts newspaper opposed him in 1958. Most of the newspapers in 1958 had actually endorsed his reelection, including the Republican newspapers. He won 73.6 percent (1,362,926) of the votes which gave him a margin of 874,608 over his opponent, Vincent Celeste.

After analyzing his overwhelming victory, Kennedy determined that the presidency was within his grasp. On January 2, 1960, he called a news conference in the Senate Caucus Room and declared his candidacy for the Democratic Presidential nomination. Immediately afterwards the press circulated stories that Kennedy's real goal was the vice presidency. In a conversation with Associated Press reporter Jack Bell, Kennedy said, "I wish you'd take those goddamn words out of your typewriter because I'm never going to take second place."

In order to overcome the religious issue, he decided to enter the primaries. The primary route was reasoned as the best way to prove the electability of a youthful Catholic and to build momentum.

Primaries

Out of the sixteen states that had primaries in 1960, Kennedy entered seven and won them all. The Wisconsin and West Virginia victories were the most significant to Kennedy. He was careful not to offend favorite sons in particular regions, which accounted for his reasoning not to enter all primaries. The states in which he won were as follows: New Hampshire; Indiana; Wisconsin; West Virginia; Nebraska; Maryland; and Oregon. How did he invoke the media's influence in these victories?

Kennedy's friendly attitude toward the press in general contributed to his success. After disembarking from his plane for a campaign stop in Wisconsin, Kennedy greeted Theodore White, "Hi. Hi, Teddy, I heard you were writing a book about the campaign. Is Pierre treating you all right?" Would Richard Nixon ask a reporter how his press secretary was treating him? Never.

Kennedy and his entourage simply dazzled the media. In the race between Kennedy and Humphrey in Wisconsin, Kennedy created the most newsworthy activity. As recorded by Theodore White in *The Making of the President 1960*, the events that fascinated the press were as follows:

> ... in the flight of his personal plane, the Mother Ship; with the candidate's glamourous family; with his revolving circus

of Ivy league performers and organizers. The press, charmed by Kennedy, entranced by the purr of his political machinery, slowly fastened on the candidate from Massachusetts as the winner.

In Wisconsin, Kennedy and Humphrey spent about the same amount of campaign funds: $150,000. Despite spending the same money, Humphrey complained that he felt "like an independent merchant competing against a chain store" because Kennedy family members blitzed across the state to campaign for their brother. Since they all looked and talked the same, the Kennedys often confused the media as to which one was John. Reports that John Kennedy was campaigning in as many as three or four different places at the same time only distressed Humphrey. Wherever the Kennedy's went, the media followed.

In an effort to influence the media, Kennedy distributed his campaign book entitled *The Strategy of Peace*. The compilation of speeches mostly emphasized his stand on foreign policy. In the spring of 1960, he sent out a mass mailing of the book with the purpose of wooing the nation's intellectuals. Many of the following personages received copies of the book: editors, scientists, columnists, educators, reporters, authors, publishers, labor leaders, clergymen, public opinion leaders and liberal politicians. *The Strategy of Peace* defined Kennedy's political beliefs and, for this reason, was delivered to influential Americans with the hope that they would spread its message which would then filter through the media to the voting public. One previously pro-Humphrey professor wrote Kennedy and observed, "*The Strategy of Peace* is uncontestably the best campaign document I can imagine, for it communicates what various other books and most news reports inadequately convey.... You emerge from the book as the kind of reflective and purposeful candidate that many of us seek."

Not all Kennedy efforts to manipulate the media were successful. For example, Ambassador Kennedy attempted to convince six New York City and state Democratic leaders, because of the religious "handicap," to issue a statement to the press in which they would declare the senator as the West Virginia winner if he won at least 35 percent of its vote. The ambassador lunched with the six leaders at a restaurant in Central Park to persuade them of this. When only one agreed, he told the others, "You can go to blazes."

In West Virginia, John Kennedy falsely manipulated his image to portray himself as cast from the same mold as Franklin D. Roosevelt. FDR had been instrumental in promoting legislation that allowed coal miners to organize and earn fair wages; needless to say, he was held in high esteem in West Virginia. Kennedy called Franklin Roosevelt Jr. into the state to campaign on his behalf and invoke the image of his father to the voters. As FDR Jr. traveled the state, he held up two fingers adjoined during speeches and said, "My father and Jack Kennedy's father were just like this!"

Campaign assistants of Kennedy's asked the press to use the senator's initials when reporting in order to associate JFK with FDR. Was this image portrayal to the press genuine? After Kennedy became president, he was asked about the similarity often drawn in the press between Roosevelt and himself. He answered, "There is no validity to the comparison."

1960 Democratic National Convention

While traveling from state to state for different primaries, Kennedy often checked with his aides to see how his best-selling book, *Profiles in Courage*, was selling at the local bookstores. Frequently, he heard that it was sold out. The senator would then instruct Kenneth O'Donnell to contact his publisher to have him re-supply a stock of the books wherever he went campaigning. Even with this preparation, many of the bookstores in Los Angeles during the convention reported sell-outs of both *Profiles In Courage* and *The Strategy of Peace*.

During the Chicago Convention in 1956 when Kennedy battled Kefauver for the vice presidential nomination, the Kennedy communication system broke down between Kennedy floor lieutenants and the off-floor command center. Learning from this valuable lesson, Kennedy at the 1960 Democratic Convention organized a sophisticated electronic media command center using walkie-talkies and independently connected telephones.

The telephones connected the Kennedy headquarters, located in a cottage adjacent to the Los Angeles Sports Arena, with key people on the convention floor. Direct lines were connected with the chairs of friendly delegations (Massachusetts, Illinois, Michigan, New York, Wyoming, and Rhode Island). Floor managers Robert Kennedy and Governor Ribicoff controlled the flow of information. By establishing this communication system, Kennedy leaders could swiftly deliver any important information or handle any last minute problems.

Numerous Stevenson campaign aides later complained that the Kennedy walkie-talkies were powerful enough to monitor their radio communications on the convention floor. This telephone and radio communications system at the convention demonstrated the mastery the Kennedy forces had over their own electronic media.

After his son won the Democratic nomination on the first ballot, Ambassador Kennedy left Los Angeles and jetted back to New York. Upon arrival he phoned Henry Luce, Editor-In-Chief of Time, Inc. and arranged a dinner with him that evening at the editor's home in Manhattan.

Kennedy Sr. and Luce were friends who had exchanged favors over the years. As mentioned previously, Luce had written the introduction to John's book, *Why England Slept*. The ambassador had hired Luce's son, Hank, as special assistant to the chairman (Kennedy Sr. at the time) of the Securities and Exchange Commission.

Following dinner, Kennedy and Luce watched on TV John Kennedy's acceptance speech delivered at the Los Angeles Coliseum. Knowing that the *Time* and *Life* magazines did not support his son's candidacy, the ambassador strove to neutralize them for the upcoming campaign against Nixon. Luce acknowledged that the Democratic nominee would run as a liberal on domestic issues in order to win votes in the large liberal northern cities, and he had no quarrel with that. The editor then warned that should Kennedy's son show any weakness in defending democracy against communism throughout the world, his magazines would go after him. The ambassador assured Luce that this would not occur. Thankful for *Time's* and *Life's* neutrality during the campaign, Kennedy Sr. invited Luce — who accepted — to sit with him in attendance at the Kennedy Inaugural ball.

Campaign Against Nixon

In the media battle between Kennedy and Richard M. Nixon, Kennedy won the affection and the respect of the working correspondents while Nixon did not. His attitude toward the media won them over. Theodore White once remarked that for a reporter to be transferred from the Nixon campaign to the Kennedy campaign ". . . was as if one were transformed in the role from leper and outcast to friend and battle companion."

Nixon's fear that the press distrusted and disliked him became a self-fulfilling prophecy. White calculated that the

The Presidential Race

reporters assigned to Nixon at the beginning of the campaign were probably split 50-50 between those warm and those frosty toward him. By the end of the campaign, nearly all of the press that covered Nixon became antagonistic toward him. The antagonism resulted from the abusive treatment that they received from Nixon and his staff.

As Nixon prepared to kick his campaign into full swing, he entered Walter Reed Hospital from August 29th to September 9th to recover from an infection in his knee. Restless after his convalescence, he resumed campaigning with such extreme vigor that he exhausted the press corps following him. By criss-crossing the country so often, he gave the press little time to meet their deadlines, which put them in the uncomfortable position of having to write stories without sufficient time to digest some of the more complicated issues presented in his speeches. Nixon's indifference to the press' problems stemmed from his belief that they were out to "get him" anyway.

The rigorous travels of both candidates wore out the press. Correspondents assigned to them were often replaced and rotated to keep them fresh. In contrast to Nixon, Kennedy and his staff sympathized with the plight of the press. Whenever a correspondent joined or rejoined the Kennedy campaign, Kennedy press aides showed genuine elation toward the new team member. The aides would also slip the new press member some topical campaign information which was tailored for the interest of his particular newspaper or magazine.

Reporters following Kennedy received transcripts immediately following each of his speeches. Kennedy aides did this to allow reporters time to relax and listen without the burden of note taking. When Theodore White asked a Nixon aide why they did not provide transcripts, the aide replied, "Stuff the bastards. They're all against Dick anyway. Make them work — we aren't going to hand out prepared remarks; let them get their pencils out and listen and take notes." This policy of withholding transcripts was counterproductive, and, to aggravate the situation, the Nixon staff caused more resentment by verbally telling reporters about this policy. Finally realizing how they were only hurting themselves by forcing harassed reporters to write last minute stories, Nixon's staff later in the campaign followed Kennedy's example and began distributing transcripts after each Nixon speech.

Another key difference between the two candidates was in their accessability to the media. Kennedy's open-door policy with reporters was practiced throughout his political career. During the late fifties when the senator's popularity was blooming, his secretary, Mrs. Lincoln, complained about all the newspaper, magazine, radio, and television people seeking interviews. "Should I try to discourage them so you won't be interrupted so much?" she asked the senator. "By no means Mrs. Lincoln," Kennedy replied. "If I know one thing, it is that a politician can kill himself faster by playing hard-to-get with the press than he can by jumping off the capitol dome. And besides, I used to be a newspaperman myself. As long as they want to talk to me, I want to talk to them. Maybe longer."

Nixon's policy with reporters was to maintain a distance from them. In *The Making of the President 1960*, White — while discussing Nixon — used a disclaimer, saying that he and most other correspondents were never granted private interviews with the enigmatic Nixon.

Nixon's approach to influencing the press was quite different from Kennedy's. Nixon's strategy was to woo support from the publishers of newspapers, and he was successful at it. In 1960, he was endorsed by 78 percent of all newspapers whose publishers took a stand. Additionally, he

The Presidential Race

won the editorial support of all mass magazines whose owners endorsed candidates. Kennedy's approach was to win the favor of the reporters — the ones who actually wrote all the stories. The senator hoped that their favorable bias would seep into the reports filed in the many Republican controlled publications.

Kennedy actually enjoyed the company of reporters. He flattered them by asking their advice on issues, though he rarely observed it, and he borrowed their combs and pencils when pressed for time. The senator once convinced Theodore White, traveling with him on his private plane the *Caroline*, to redraft a campaign brochure by saying, "You're the only professional writer on the plane, and you're getting free booze." Kennedy discarded the redraft and told White that its style was not hard enough.

Usually, after a candidate made a political appearance, his assistants gave the press a crowd estimate. The temptation existed, of course, for them to overestimate in order to make their candidate seem more popular. Image-conscious Kennedy aides once announced that a Kennedy rally netted some 35,000 attendees, a figure that seemed extremely high by reporters on the scene. When later questioned by about a half dozen reporters about this sensitive subject, Kennedy defused the issue by joking about how Pierre "Plucky" Salinger arrived at the crowd estimate: "Plucky counts the nuns, and then multiplies them by 100." By using his disarming humor, Kennedy influenced the press into killing a potentially damaging story about the crowd estimates.

It can be generally assumed that Kennedy's relationship with the press did contribute to his ultimate victory over Nixon. Since the winning margin of the popular vote was so narrow (one-tenth of one percent), every favorable factor for Kennedy looms larger in retrospect.

At a time in the future, Bob Woodward and Carl Bernstein

were searching through the *Washington Post* office trying to obtain information from anyone who had more than superficial contact with members of the Nixon White House staff. They mentioned their expectations were not high, given the relationship between Nixon and the press. In *All the President's Men*, Woodward and Bernstein reminisced: "That heady era of good feeling, in which reporters had rubbed elbows and shoulders with President Kennedy's men in touch football and candlelit backyards in Georgetown and Cleveland Park, was a thing of the past."

NOTES

43
"Jack Kennedy has left": "Man Out Front," *Time*, Vol. LXX, No. 23, December 2, 1957, p. 17.

43
During this time: Theodore C. Sorensen, *Kennedy* (New York: Bantam Books, Inc., 1965), p. 119.

43
"We're going to sell Jack": Richard J. Whalen, *The Founding Father — The Story of Joseph P. Kennedy* (New York: The New American Library of World Literature, Inc., 1964), p. 446.

43
"I'll tell you how to sell": Ibid.

43
"Mrs. Lincoln, why don't you keep": Evelyn Lincoln, *My Twelve Years With John F. Kennedy* (New York: Bantam Books, Inc., 1965), p. 80.

44
"You would be surprised": Rose Kennedy, *Times To Remember* (Garden City, New York: Doubleday & Company, Inc., 1974), p. 262.

45
In Massachusetts: Kenneth P. O'Donnell, David F. Powers, and Joe McCarthy, *"Johnny, We Hardly Knew Ye"* (Boston: Little, Brown and Company, 1970), pp. 144f.

45
John Kennedy realized his goal: Details of Kennedy's 1958 senate reelection results in O'Donnell, Powers, and McCarthy, pp. 145f.

46
"I wish you'd take": Ralph G. Martin, *A Hero For Our Time — An Intimate Story of the Kennedy Years* (New York: Macmillan Publishing Company, 1983), p. 124.

46
"Hi. Hi, Teddy": Theodore H. White, *In Search of History* (New York: Warner Books, 1978), p. 456.

46
". . . in the flight of his personal plane": Theodore H. White, *The Making Of The President 1960* (New York: Atheneum House, Inc., 1961) p. 112.

47
"like an independent merchant": Sorensen, p. 152.

47
In an effort to influence: Details about *The Strategy of Peace* are in Sorensen, pp. 133f.

47
"The Strategy of Peace is uncontestably": Ibid., p. 134.

48
"You can go to blazes.": Whalen, p. 452.

48
"My father and Jack Kennedy's father": Michael R. Beschloss, *Kennedy and Roosevelt — The Uneasy Alliance* (New York: W.W. Norton & Company, 1980), p. 276.

48
"There is no validity": Whalen, p. 460.

49
During the Chicago Convention: See White, *The Making Of The President 1960*, p. 182.

49
After his son won: David Halberstam, *The Best and the Brightest* (New York: Random House, 1969), pp. 18f.

50
". . . was as if one were transformed": White, *The Making Of The President 1960*, p. 378.

50
White calculated: Ibid.

51
The aides would also slip: Ibid., p. 379.

51
"Stuff the bastards": Ibid., p. 377.

52
"Should I try to discourage them": Lincoln, p. 15.

52
Nixon's approach to influencing: See White, *The Making Of The President 1960*, p. 378.

53
"You're the only professional writer": White, *In Search Of History*, p. 461.

53
"Plucky counts the nuns": Benjamin C. Bradlee, *Conversations With Kennedy* (New York: Pocket Books, 1976), p. 19.

54
"That heady era of good feeling": Carl Bernstein and Bob Woodward, *All The President's Men* (New York: Warner Books, 1974), p. 131.

4

Kennedy vs. the Media

"If you run that story, I may wind up buying *Look* magazine."

—President Kennedy to a *Look* magazine editor

Despite all of Kennedy's overatures and cooperation with the media, they sometimes wrote or aired reports with which he disagreed. Significantly, he would then contact the source via a phone call, letter, or staff person to let them know of his displeasure and to seek "corrections."

The press was aware of Kennedy's ever watchful eye over what they wrote. In order to augment his monitoring ability, Kennedy in 1954 enrolled in a speed reading course taught in Baltimore. At a rate of 1200 words a minute, he would read more than a half dozen newspapers a day. Whenever Kennedy read a favorable article about himself on the presidential campaign trail, he would not only tell the writer that he had read it, but would then from memory quote some of its direct phrases. "Any time you think no one in Washington is reading you," a Portland, Maine publisher once told a newly hired editor, "put in a good word about Senator Kennedy, and you'll get a letter the next week."

Sometimes news articles were unfavorable. "Get Sorensen," Senator Kennedy would tell his secretary after reading a story that he did not agree with. "Ted, look at what this fellow has said about me. Let's give him the facts and blast him." The reporter soon thereafter would receive a letter from the Kennedy office refuting the offensive passages. If the reporter in future articles maintained his point of view, Kennedy would not send a second letter. He would just say, "His mind's made up and facts won't change it."

One time, Drew Pearson appeared on television and charged that Kennedy had not written *Profiles In Courage*. Several sources, after the publication of the book indicated that it was written, more or less, as a group effort. To denounce Pearson's claim, the senator sent his collection of notes, drafts, and dictabelt tapes of his voice used in writing the book to his personal lawyer, Clark Clifford. Threatening a lawsuit, Kennedy obtained a retraction. By carefully examining the notes and tapes held in the Kennedy Library in Massachusetts, author Herbert Parmet has determined that they are extremely lacking in completeness and continuity, suggesting that Kennedy may not have been the sole author.

After declaring himself a candidate for the presidency, Kennedy still was nagged continually by reporters to admit that he really sought only the vice presidency because of his youth. Immediately before the 1960 Democratic Convention, Stewart Alsop interviewed Kennedy about this issue.

> Alsop: I think that the most likely alternative would be a Stevenson-Kennedy ticket if you don't make it and Johnson and Symington don't make it. My God, the pressure you must be under from Stevenson.
> Kennedy (who was agitated by the question): Look, I'll make you an offer — if I take the vice presidency under anybody, I'll send you a check the next day for $25,000.

When Alsop phoned Kennedy's senate office to ask permission to print the interview in the "Keeping Posted" section of the *Saturday Evening Post*, Kennedy agreed under one condition. Revising the transcript he crossed out "send you a check the next day for $25,000" and replaced it with "give you my next year's Senate salary." There was no need to raise the money issue during the Democratic Convention.

Kennedy grew weary of the press referring to him in stories as "Jack." The nickname, he thought, made people still think of him as too youthful. On January 5, 1961, the *New York Times* printed a story entitled, "Kennedy Prefers 'J.F.K.' To 'Jack' For Headlines." Pierre Salinger in Palm Beach told reporters that the president-elect actually preferred either just "Kennedy" or "JFK" in headlines. Salinger continued,

"But he also feels that the choice is up to the newspapers." Suddenly, many papers began referring to him as "JFK" — at least those that wanted a good standing with the White House.

Just prior to the top secret Bay of Pigs invasion, Gilbert Harrison of the *New Republic* sent Arthur Schlesinger Jr. (then special assistant to the president) a draft entitled "Our Men in Miami," which they considered publishing. Apparently, the CIA-trained Cuban exiles talked to the press prior to the supposedly secret invasion about how they would receive United States recognition as they fought to free their homeland. Perturbed by all this, Schlesinger showed the article to Kennedy who wanted it stopped. At the president's request, Harrison chose not to run the article.

Concurrently, the *New York Times* prepared a story on the impending invasion. This time the president personally called James Reston, with the *Times*, to have the story killed for national security reasons. The *Times* decided not to print the story fearing that they might alert Castro and cause casualties or might even cause the administration to cancel the mission, thereby interfering with national policy.

Shortly after the disastrous invasion, Kennedy gave a speech entitled, "The President and the Press," before the American Publishers Association in New York City. In it he called for "the need for far greater secrecy." He asked members of the press to "reexamine their own responsibilities" and to ask themselves not only whether a story is newsworthy, but ask, "Is it in the interest of the national security?" After Kennedy had some time to reevaluate the whole Bay of Pigs debacle, he indicated to aides that he wished the press had ignored his censorship and printed the articles. "If the story had appeared before the invasion," he said, "I might have had second thoughts about it — I might have called it off."

Throughout his political career, Kennedy displayed a passion for image control. He absolutely refused to be photographed wearing a hat whenever he could avoid it. His friends urged him to wear a hat during his first congressional race to look older, but he refused and said that he did not want to appear as a typical hat-wearing, hands-over-head-waving Boston politician. As senator, he was elected to the Harvard Board of Overseers which required that he wear a top hat at Harvard's commencement exercises. Since it was a great honor to be appointed, he reluctantly ordered the required hat. His secretary, Mrs. Lincoln, remembered the day he rushed to the mirror to try on the hat as soon as he received it. Looking like a young boy dressed in his first "grown-up" clothes, Kennedy worked at his desk the remainder of the afternoon and never once removed the top hat.

Playing golf and using crutches for his bad back also made him camera shy. Crutches implied weakness, while golf playing evoked images of Eisenhower's sluggish country club days at the White House where he dented the floors with his golf shoe spikes.

Not only was Kennedy overly concerned about pictures taken of him, but he became extremely upset whenever a publication printed an untruth about him. One day Hugh Sidey from *Time* magazine was at the White House when the president discovered a blatant error in *Time*. Sidey was there on February 20, 1962 with the press corps to share and record the experience of John Glenn's completion of his first orbit in space. On this wondrous day, Kenneth O'Donnell barged into the press room to grab Sidey because the president wanted to have a word with him in the Oval Office. As it turned out, *Time*, in its "People" section, had printed a piece that claimed JFK had posed for *Gentleman's Quarterly*, a men's fashion magazine. Outraged, Kennedy chastised Sidey as he pointed to a copy of *Time*.

"This goddamn magazine is just too much. Where did you get this ridiculous item about me?" complained Kennedy in a roomful of aides as he prepared to congratulate John Glenn on the phone upon his successful return to earth. Sidey, not noticing the seriousness on Kennedy's face began to laugh, which only infuriated the president:

> What do you mean I posed for them? What do you mean? Why did you do this? I never posed for them. I'll be the laughingstock of the country. They'll remember me as the man who posed for *Gentleman's Quarterly*. People always remember the wrong things, they remember Arthur Godfrey for buzzing a tower and Calvin Coolidge for wearing those hats and they'll remember me for this.

Quickly interrupting, Admiral Tazewell Shepherd, Kennedy's naval aide, informed the president that Glenn was now on the phone aboard the U.S.S. *Noa*. Before picking up the phone Kennedy continued, "Sidey you son of a bitch, see if you can get this right."

> The President: Hello?
> Colonel Glenn: Hello Sir.
> The President: Colonel?
> Colonel Glenn: This is Colonel Glenn.
> The President: Listen, Colonel, we are really proud of you, and I must say you did a wonderful job.
> Colonel Glenn: Thanks, Mr. President.
> The President: We are glad you got down in very good shape. I have been watching your father and mother on television, and they seemed very happy.
> Colonel Glenn: It was a wonderful trip — almost unbelievable, thinking back on it right now. But it was really tremendous.

The President: Well, I am coming down to Canaveral on Friday, and hope you will come up to Washington on Monday or Tuesday, and we will be looking forward to seeing you there.
Colonel Glenn: Fine. I will certainly look forward to it.

Not skipping a beat, Kennedy hung up the phone and turned again to Sidey, "You sons of bitches, you always do this to me. That damn magazine of yours!" While Sidey did not appreciate being berated, he considered it worth the temporary embarrassment to have the close access to the president of the United States.

In another fit of anger JFK once cancelled the twenty-four subscriptions of the Republican *New York Herald Tribune* delivered to the White House. Kennedy was irritated because a front page story in the paper implied Democratic involvement on the congressional investigation of Billie Sol Estes, while ignoring another investigation of Eisenhower cabinet members involved in a copper stockpiling scandal. Lyndon Johnson's relationship with Estes was being examined at that time, as well; Estes was later convicted for scheming to defraud some large financial investment firms.

Complaining to Benjamin Bradlee of *Newsweek*, Kennedy referred to the fact that the *Tribune* did not even mention the stockpiling scandal and said, "... those bastards didn't even have a line on it. Not a goddamn line." He then rationalized to Bradlee that John Hay Whitney, publisher of the *Herald Tribune*, kept the paper alive in order to help Nelson Rockefeller's presidential aspirations for 1964. Kennedy suggested that Bradlee convince Philip Graham, publisher of the *Washington Post*, to purchase the *Tribune*. The paper's subscription was renewed when the president realized his staff bought copies at newsstands during the embargo.

While President Kennedy normally sought publicity, there

were times when he needed his privacy. He often went sailing to relax and escape the pressures of the White House. Kennedy was known to purposely turn his back whenever he saw photographers patrolling on boats in his vicinity. One windy day he sailed back to harbor and hit the wharf so hard that the mast fell and the rigging collapsed. To his dismay, stories about the event appeared in the press. "What are you bastards trying to do to me?" he queried Larry Newman. "What do you think the Republicans are going to do when the commander-in-chief can't even get a sailboat ashore?" After further reflection on the incident, Kennedy phoned Newman. "I think you're right. I've been looking at it from a political sense. The people will look on me as a human being."

In March of 1962, Jacqueline Kennedy took a goodwill trip to India in an attempt to smooth relations between the U.S. and India after the latter's seizure of the island of Goa. About a hundred news reporters followed her there to cover the trip. Everything went well until after the trip when *Newsweek* ran a story asserting that Jacky had spent too much time touring with the Prime Minister and seeing the country's most famous sites (e.g. Taj Mahal) rather than visiting the poverty-stricken areas of India. Bitterly disappointed in the magazine's coverage of the trip, the president phoned Benjamin Bradlee to voice his complaint:

> That wasn't one of your best efforts, was it? She's really broken her ass on this trip, and you can always find some broken-down Englishman or some NBC stringer to knock anything. I don't get all this crap about how she should've been rubbing her nose in the grinding poverty of India. When the French invite you to Paris, they don't show you the sewers; they take you to Versailles.

In a later conversation with Bradlee, Kennedy added the following:

> When we have distinguished visitors, we take them to Mount Vernon; we don't take them to some abandoned coal mine in West Virginia. Ken Galbraith (then U.S. Ambassador to India) told me that Jacky took all the bitterness out of our relations with India. If I had gone, we would have talked about Kashmir and Goa. But Jacky did a hell of a job.

One evening, the president appeared on live television on a news program and was questioned by three White House correspondents. Watching it at home, Benjamin Bradlee felt threatened by seeing the TV program come off so well, much better he thought than a written version would have been. After the program, Bradlee phoned Kennedy to compliment him on his performance. Mindful of how the press enjoyed editorializing, Kennedy responded, "Well, I always said that when we don't have to go through you bastards, we can really get our story to the American people."

Despite all the criticism Bradlee took from Kennedy, they were actually good friends. When Kennedy came to Los Angeles for the 1956 convention and to West Virginia to make his victory speech, Bradlee flew with him. Many correspondents envied Bradlee's inside connection to the White House; often Bradlee would get information that other reporters would not, which would appear in the "Periscope" section of *Newsweek*. Their relationship could be termed as mutually beneficial since they would often share information that normally would not be exchanged between the executive branch and the press.

As a favor to his father, President Kennedy championed the appointment of Francis X. Morrissey, a friend of the ambassador's, to a federal judgeship. The opportunity became available to Morrissey when Kennedy passed a bill creating seventy-three new federal judgeships. Since Morrissey — a municipal court judge — did not have a law degree, he was found unqualified by the American Bar Association, the Massachusetts Bar Association, and the Boston Bar Association. Critical of the proposed appointment, *Newsweek* let its disapproval be known in a news story. Again angered at the magazine, Kennedy phoned Bradlee.

"Jesus Christ, you guys are something else. When I was elected, you all said that my old man would run the country in consultation with the pope. Now here's the only thing he's ever asked me to do for him, and you guys piss all over me." As resistance mounted against Morrissey, the president quietly withdrew his support and the appointment was never approved.

What also disturbed Kennedy during his administration was the number of leaks that trickled to the press. To his chagrin, he sometimes found that he had inadvertently caused them. Determined to find the source of one leak, he sent Press Secretary Pierre Salinger to investigate the situation. Salinger hunted for two days seeking to find the source of a premature news leak about the planned Cuban embargo. Reporting back to the president, Salinger said that he found the source. Kennedy asked, "Who was it?" "You," said Salinger, "Didn't you tell George Smathers (Florida senator and friend of Kennedy's)?" When Kennedy affirmed that he had indeed told Smathers, Salinger continued, "Well, George told a friend of his on the *Tampa Tribune* and that was that."

One final episode that involved Kennedy's conflict with the press was a story referred to as "John's Other Wife" — his alleged previous marriage to a two-time divorcee. In 1956, the published Blauvelt family genealogy contained a passage stating, "Durie (Malcolm) then married John F. Kennedy, son of Joseph P. Kennedy, onetime ambassador to England. There were no children . . . ." Kennedy and Durie Malcolm had in fact dated in 1947. Their respective families were neighbors at the time in Palm Beach. During their dating period, a newspaper story observed, "She is beautiful and intelligent. A tiny obstacle is that the Kennedy clan frowns on divorce." As rumors continued to spread, the president commented that the story was "too ridiculous to deny."

The "other wife" story got out of control when *Look* magazine prepared to do a piece on it. Brandishing the power available to a millionaire president, Kennedy sternly warned one of its editors, "If you run that story, I may wind up buying *Look* magazine." The editor soberly responded, "That sounds like a threat." Kennedy also ordered his lawyer to inform the *New York Daily News* that they could publish the story "at their peril." Due to the growing rumors spreading, the president finally allowed *Newsweek* to run a story on the alleged "other wife."

Benjamin Bradlee noted that some anti-Semitic, racist hate sheets had previously printed articles about the story ("Kennedy's Divorce Exposed! Is Present Marriage Valid? Excommunication Possible"). Bradlee told Pierre Salinger that in order for *Newsweek* to investigate the matter adequately, they would need FBI documentation about the background of the publications and individuals responsible for printing the Blauvelt story. Remarkably, Kennedy agreed to this under one condition: the completed story must be approved by him. The deal was struck, so Bradlee and an assistant were given the material to read for only twenty-four hours under the stipulation that it could not be photocopied, and the reporters could not admit that they had seen the FBI files. The *Newsweek* correspondents that interviewed

Kennedy for the story were puzzled that "he never flatly denied it."

Publically, Kennedy appeared to get along with the media better than any other previous president. But behind the scenes, they were always at odds with each other. The president did not communicate closely with the press simply for the purpose of trying to make the news more favorable to him; he desired to make the news more objective and accurate. Sometimes, Kennedy thought that the press deliberately printed misinformation, and every time he would ask for corrections, they would charge him with news managing. After reading a *Look* story concerning his practice of phoning various reporters to complain about unfavorable articles, Kennedy sniffed, "This is the best example of paranoia I have seen from these fellows yet."

Kennedy was involved in a love-hate relationship with the media. He confided in Arthur Schlesinger that he found out more about the events in Vietnam from reporters than he did from his generals and ambassadors.

NOTES

59
In order to augment: Details of Kennedy's reading ability are in Arthur M. Schlesinger Jr., *A Thousand Days* (New York: Fawcett Premier Books, 1965), p. 104. See also Evelyn Lincoln, *My Twelve Years With John F. Kennedy* (New York: Bantam Books, Inc., 1965), p. 43 and p. 202.

59
"Any time you think": Theodore C. Sorensen, *Kennedy* (New York: Bantam Books, Inc., 1965), p. 357.

59
"Get Sorensen": Lincoln, pp. 15f.

59
One time, Drew Pearson appeared: Details on the writing of *Profiles In Courage* are in the following: Garry Wills, *The Kennedy Imprisonment* (Boston: Little, Brown and Company, 1981), pp. 134ff.; Richard J. Whalen, *The Founding Father — The Story of Joseph P. Kennedy* (New York: The New American Library of World Literature, Inc., 1964), pp. 442f.; and Schlesinger, p. 118.

60
"Alsop: I think that the most": Lincoln, p. 116.

60
"send you a check the next day": Ibid.

60
"Kennedy Prefers 'J.F.K.' ": Gene Brown (ed.), *The Kennedys — A New York Times Profile* (New York: Arno Press, 1980), p. 60.

61
Just prior to the top secret: See Schlesinger, pp. 244f. and Ralph G. Martin, *A Hero For Our Time — An Intimate Story of the Kennedy Years* (New York: Macmillan Publishing Company, 1983), pp. 327ff.

61
"The President and the Press": See the complete text of the speech in John F. Kennedy, *Public Papers of the Presidents of the United States (1961)* (Washington, D.C.: United States Government Printing Office, 1962), pp. 334ff.

61
"If the story had appeared": Martin, p. 327.

62
His secretary, Mrs. Lincoln: See Lincoln, p. 87.

63
"This goddamn magazine is just too much.": David Halberstam, *The Powers That Be* (New York: Dell Publishing Company, 1979), pp. 505f.
63
"The President: Hello?": John F. Kennedy, *Public Papers of the Presidents of the United States (1962)* (Washington, D.C.: United States Government Printing Office, 1963), p. 150.
64
In another fit of anger: See Sorensen, p. 355.
64
". . . those bastards didn't even": Benjamin C. Bradlee, *Conversations With Kennedy* (New York: Pocket Books, 1976), p. 96.
65
"What are you bastards": Martin, p. 374.
65
"That wasn't one of your best efforts": Bradlee, p. 65.
66
"When we have distinguished visitors": Ibid., p. 70.
66
"Well, I always said": Ibid., p. 123.
67
"Jesus Christ, you guys": Ibid., p. 23.
67
"Who was it?": Ibid., p. 56.
67
One final episode: Details of Kennedy's "other wife" story are in Martin, pp. 399f. and Bradlee, pp. 108ff.
68
"If you run that story": Martin, p. 399.

69
"he never flatly denied it": Ibid., p. 400.

69
The president did not communicate: See Sorensen, pp. 356ff.

69
"This is the best example": Schlesinger, p. 659.

69
He confided in Arthur Schlesinger: David Halberstam, *The Best and the Brightest* (New York: Random House, 1969), p. 94.

5

Communication Style: A Montage of Images

"... Attention to details, even the minor gestures that are part of human communication, is important in all human relationships."

— Rose Kennedy

When people recall the Kennedy administration, do they remember the style or the substance? Do they remember that Kennedy backed the first signing of a limited Nuclear Test Ban Treaty with the Soviet Union, or do they remember his bad back and famous rocking chair? Do they remember that he, for the first time on television, participated in The Great Debates with Richard Nixon, or do they remember the great beauty and culture of his wife Jacqueline? Do people remember that he had an eye for establishing the Peace Corps, raising the minimum wage, increasing aid to education, or do they remember that he had an eye for the ladies?

The Kennedy administration will be remembered for many achievements, but its style may well overshadow its substance. Television shifted peoples' attention from issues, and caused them to focus on the more personal qualities of a candidate, his ability to speak, and his style of presentation. In this chapter, Kennedy's relationships with individuals and groups will be surveyed, his communication style will be explored.

The low opinion that people had about politics and politicians concerned Kennedy. In his characteristically humorous style he once joked, "Mothers may still want their favorite sons to grow up to be President, but . . . they do not want them to become politicians in the process." Since politics was his business, he did his utmost to enhance its image. In a more serious moment, Kennedy transcribed his thoughts on public service:

> . . . the fact remains that politics has become one of our most abused and neglected professions. It is this profession, it is these politicians who make the great decision of war and peace, prosperity and recession, the decisions as to whether

we look to the future or the past. In a large sense everything new depends on what the government decides. Therefore, if you are interested, if you want to participate, if you feel strongly about any public question, whether it is labor, what happens in India, the future of American agriculture, whatever it may be, it seems to me that governmental service is the way to translate this interest into action, that the natural place for the concerned citizen is to contribute part of his life to the national interest.

Although he spent a large part of his life suffering from illnesses, he strove to project an image of health, youth, and vigor. In this respect, his style was similar to that of President Theodore Roosevelt, who became America's youngest ever president following the assasination of President McKinley (Kennedy was the youngest ever elected president). Roosevelt grew up as a nearsighted asthmatic child with a frail body. By his own resolve, Roosevelt undertook a regiment of strenuous exercises and adventures to strengthen his body.

During his lifetime, Kennedy's illnesses included scarlet fever, jaundice, malaria, and an adrenalin insufficiency; he also suffered from a bad back which required three operations. Young Bobby Kennedy once joked, "If a mosquito bit Jack Kennedy, the mosquito would die." Rejected by the Army because of his back condition after volunteering in the spring of 1941, Kennedy undertook back strengthening exercises and was later accepted by the Navy and went on to captain the famous PT-109. During his administration, Kennedy promoted physical fitness through the Presidential Fitness Awards Program and the Youth Fitness Program. His style of showing strength and downplaying weakness characterized his career in public service.

Kennedy, perhaps America's vainest president, went to

great lengths to demonstrate health and strength. On one occasion the president was meeting with two aides in his office when his secretary Mrs. Lincoln handed him two cold pills with his coffee. He hastily stuffed the pills into his pocket, letting Mrs. Lincoln know that he did not wish to advertise his affliction. Self-conscious about his reading glasses, he would rarely wear them in public. As senator and president, Kennedy would privately use his crutches to ease his chronic back pain while walking. During the periods when he was using his crutches, he would hide them before a visitor entered his office.

When barnstorming the country, Kennedy usually appeared before crowds hatless and coatless, regardless of the weather. Then there is the paradigm example of his displaying strength despite his condition. On Inauguration Day, January 20, 1961, the city of Washington, D.C. endured 7.7 inches of newly fallen snow, fierce winds, and a sub-freezing temperature of 22 degrees Fahrenheit. Facing these frigid conditions, Kennedy was pictured hatless and overcoatless on the cover of *The New York Times*. In its coverage of the event, the *Times* on January 21, 1961 described Kennedy's garb: "Mr. Kennedy who is usually hatless, seemed self-consciously uncomfortable in his topper (top hat). He wore it as briefly as possible on the trips back and forth from the White House to Capitol Hill. He also shed his coat frequently in the long day outdoors."

*

Once elected president, Kennedy spent the few months prior to the inauguration searching frantically for aides who would reflect his style. Expressing his sentiment about how a potential aide voted, he said, "Now on those key jobs, I don't care whether a man is a Democrat or an Igorot. I want the best fellow I can get for the particular job." In his book, David Halberstam sarcastically referred to the aides as "The Best and the Brightest" as he pointed out their faults and foibles. Nonetheless, Kennedy earnestly wanted people who were respected leaders in their fields.

Some preferred traits in potential aides included: being youthful, self-confident, intelligent, possessing athletic looks, being an award winner (a Pulitzer Prize would do fine), vigor, and having a degree from an Ivy League school. Some definite handicaps were described by Sargent Shriver (a Kennedy brother-in-law and first Peace Corps Director): "too ideological, too earnest, too emotional, too talkative, too dull." A candidate would be doomed when Kennedy said, "He's a very common man," or "That's a very ordinary type."

The New Frontier administration bragged about its fifteen Rhodes Scholars and its large number of Yale men. Kennedy's Special Military Representative, General Maxwell Taylor, exemplified many of the characteristics that a Kennedy aide should possess. He was articulate, handsome, athletic; he spoke several languages and had written a book.

The communication style between Kennedy and his close aides was unique. Kennedy and his staff spoke in a shorthand, codelike manner with a minimal use of words; the tartness and brevity between them showed that they understood the code. Next to his brother Robert, President Kennedy's most trusted and loyal staff member was Theodore Sorensen, special counsel to the president. Kennedy once referred to him as "my intellectual blood bank." "As their relationship grew stronger," said Mrs. Lincoln, "there seemed to be a kind of unspoken communication between them. Often Ted would start to work on something with little more than a nod from the Senator."

*

After several years in politics, Kennedy became masterful at receiving people in greeting lines. On these occasions the softer side of his communication style came through. When introduced to Mrs. Kenneth O'Donnell and Mrs. David Powers (the wives of two top aides) at his wedding reception, Kennedy lavishly praised the political abilities of each woman's husband in turn and explained that without his help, he never would have been elected senator. O'Donnell and Powers complained that from then on Kennedy could do no wrong in their wive's eyes, a consequence Kennedy had clearly intended.

At one of the Kennedy Tea Parties during the first congressional race, Kennedy was greeting people in a reception line when he saw an elderly woman buck the line and skip to the front rather than waiting her turn. Kennedy watched her being escorted back; then excused himself from the reception line, found her, shook her hand, and thanked her for coming. She returned to her table, elated at having received such cordial treatment. Describing the scene, a Kennedy aide remarked, "In a situation like that you could count on Jack to do the right thing."

On another occasion, he displayed his social graces to Senator Dodd's wife. Caught up in the midst of the 1960 Presidential Primaries, Kennedy walked through the senate halls and passed Mrs. Dodd without recognizing her. Upset with his preoccupation, he dictated a note to her, "I am extremely sorry that I was in such a hurry today that I didn't recognize you. I am afraid that the same thing will happen to me with my wife one of these days. I have always had a warm feeling for you, and I was delighted to see you looking so well." The apology was hand delivered immediately by an aide. He always had a knack for just the right personal touch.

*

The issue of his personal wealth hounded Kennedy throughout his political career. Joseph Kennedy Sr. created an environment in which his children could pursue their interests and careers without having to grovel for a weekly paycheck as the common man must do.

There were always those who claimed that the Kennedy's "bought" this or that election. Kennedy usually maintained his style and wit and often made jokes about his family's money. However, mindful of his personal fortune worth millions and a presidential salary of $100,000 a year, he strove to deflect further complaints by donating his entire presidential salary to charity. As a matter of fact, he donated all his government salaries (congressional, senatorial, and presidential) to charities, an amount of approximately half a million dollars.

Always politically astute and with an eye toward reelection in 1964, he distributed the presidential salary judiciously. The 1961-1962 charity list included the following: Boy Scouts of America; Girl Scouts of America; Boys' Club of America; Girls' Club of America; Services for Crippled Children; National Association for Retarded Children; Federation of Jewish Philanthropies; St. John's Hospital (Santa Monica, Calif.); Massachusetts General Hospital; United Negro College Fund; and the Cuban Families Committee.

*

Another aspect of Kennedy's communication style was his

penchant for gift-giving to instill a sense of fellowship among his associates and friends. Mrs. Lincoln was usually put in charge of sending out the gifts. Acquaintances received *Bartlett's Quotations* (one of Kennedy's favorite books); special friends were shipped an inscribed silver bowl; and the *Congressional Cook Book*, which described the favorite recipes of the wives of congressmen and senators, was sent to benefits and bazaars.

While Senator Kennedy convalesced from his third and final back operation in Palm Beach, he turned a disadvantage into an advantage and penned *Profiles In Courage*. Upon his return to the senate, he sent out autographed copies — hand delivered by aides — to all senators. Personal friends and prominent people also received autographed copies. By distributing his Pulitzer Prize winning book, he promoted himself as an intellectual.

Gold PT-109 boat tie clips served as important gifts at the White House. These were miniature medal reproductions of Kennedy's PT-109 boat. They were helpful in reminding recipients of the president's war hero days. Recipients included close friends and astronauts; on a political trip to Africa, Ted Kennedy distributed some to important Africans. The president gave cigarette lighters to those who accompanied him on his trip abroad to Germany, Ireland, England, and Italy. Engraved on one side was, "European trip of President Kennedy, June, 1963," and on the other side was the presidential seal. After Professor Archibald Cox assisted Kennedy in drafting a bill to curb corruption in labor unions, he received as a gift a watch identical to Kennedy's own.

Perhaps the most significant momento that Kennedy distributed was a silver calendar which he gave to each individual who assisted him during the Cuban Missile Crisis. He designed the calendar himself with the month of October struck in silver on a wooden plaque with the eleven crisis days set off in different typestyle. At the top of the silver calendar the initials of the president were engraved in one corner with the recipients' initials on the other side. By extending these shared symbols of gratitude, Kennedy created a special bond between his staff members and himself.

In-Office Behavior

While discussing Robert Kennedy, Sandy Vanocur once said, ". . . there is simply no sense in being a Kennedy if you do not keep asking yourself and others to do better." John Kennedy operated his staff office under this policy as well. Kennedy's management style reflected his distaste for bureaucracies; he preferred central control over issues and created ad hoc committees to deal with problems. Kennedy's office style illuminates his communication style.

Mrs. Lincoln recalled that there was always a sense of immediacy about her boss. If he wanted something done, he wanted it done NOW. Regardless of the difficulties in his requests, he would not accept "no" as an answer. When Mrs. Lincoln said, "No, I couldn't get the reservation," he would ask why. He was not trying to be difficult; he simply believed that almost anything could be done. To secure the reservation he would ask her to call someone else or say, "Let me talk to them."

"If you proved up to the task, he called on you again," said Kennedy's secretary. "If you were slow on performance, the next time he asked someone else to do it. If he thought you were taking a little longer than necessary to get the job done, he would ask you about the delay. If you had a logical answer, he was satisfied. But if you said, 'I haven't had time to do it,' once again he would lose confidence in you."

Sometimes his persistence in believing that anything could be done would lead to humorous exchanges with his staff.

One day in the Oval Office with Pierre Salinger and Ralph Dungan present, Mrs. Lincoln looked out the window and mused, "The south lawn will look nice with deer on it." Salinger yelled, "Don't tell me they are going to put deer out there!" Dungan added, "Deer will never stay in that yard. They'll jump right over the fence." At that moment Kennedy, who had never previously considered having deer, entered the office, heard their conversation, and responded, "Why can't we have deer out there? Call the Zoo. Find out whether it would be safe for them to be there." After speaking to the Zoo officials, Mrs. Lincoln relayed to the president that deer on the South Lawn would not be practical. Hearing this, he decided against pursuing it further.

*

Kennedy was a strong believer in the power of redundancy. When requesting information or assigning speeches to his writers, he often gave the same assignment to two or three different staffers. They were generally unaware that others were working on the same project. This sytem ensured that deadlines were met should one writer be delayed, and new and different ideas could be combined to make a better speech. This was analogous to NASA's Space Shuttle system; the Shuttle required only one functioning on-board computer, but it carried five. When a reporter queried Kennedy about his practice of delegating the same assignment to different aides, he responded, "I simply cannot afford to have just one set of advisers."

*

President Kennedy received around 5,000 pieces of mail every day. After being sorted at the State Department Building, about 100 letters would reach Mrs. Lincoln's desk.

Of the remainder, every 50th unsolicited letter was taken at random and saved for the president to read. Kennedy always studied closely the letters that criticized him because he believed he learned the most from them.

Kennedy had an insatiable appetite for any news that could be of value to him. Functioning as a public relations office, his senatorial office subscribed to a newspaper clipping service. The senator also asked his staff to search through Massachusetts newspapers to clip and save interesting articles for him to read.

An important function of his public relations-like office was to keep his constituents happy. Once an Irish Boston woman, a shut-in, wrote Kennedy's senate office and asked for a free television to brighten her life. Moved by her request the senator ordered an aide to "Buy her a good used television and send it over to her. She's a poor shut-in." After she received the TV set, she mailed it right back and complained in a letter: "Never so insulted in my life. Imagine a used television set with a ten-inch screen from a man with your wealth." She then demanded that he send a new one with a twenty-one inch screen. After reading the letter with its new request, Kennedy commented, "She's not a shut-in. Somebody probably locked her in."

*

When Kennedy was growing up, displays of emotion were frowned on by his domineering father. Kennedy flared occasionally, but his anger was always short-lived. One afternoon the president was scheduled to meet with a group of people from Miss Porter's School, Jacqueline Kennedy's alma mater. But because of a mix-up, when Kennedy appeared at the Rose Garden to meet them no one was there. He returned to his office in a bad mood and later in the day

Communication Style

berated one of his staff members and scolded a newspaper reporter. A short while later he called Mrs. Lincoln into his office and dictated separate apology letters for the two he had attacked. Before his secretary left the office for home, Kennedy phoned her and said, "Mrs. Lincoln, would you see that those letters go out tonight?" While his communication style was forceful, he did not want a residue of hard feelings.

At another time, President-elect Kennedy visited the home of Larry and Sancy Newman in Hyannis Port and listened as staff members discussed their plans to isolate him from matters that they determined should not concern him as president. Drinking a Heineken and obviously upset, he warned:

> Listen you sons of bitches, I want you to remember one thing. You know there's a guy right behind each of you who's working for me. And there's a guy behind him who's working for me. So there's not a goddamn thing any one of you guys can do to keep things away from me. So if you try to pull any bullshit, the next thing you know, you'll be out.

Feeling the sudden tension in the room he asked, "How about another beer?" Interestingly, he had not yet finished his own. Once again, he showed firmness and control. Also, he let it be known that he never wanted issues bottled up in the bureaucracy of his own staff; central control was the style of his presidency.

*

Another characteristic of Kennedy's communication style was his penchant for nicknaming his associates. Pierre Salinger became "Plucky"; Inga Arvad was "Inga-Binga"; also there were Paul "Grand Old Lovable" Fay; Benjamin "Benjy" Bradlee; and a pair of White House secretaries called "Fiddle" and "Faddle."

While Kennedy enjoyed nicknaming, he was insistent about being referred to in public as "Senator" Kennedy or "Mr. President," rather than as "Jack." His obvious political "handicap" was his youth, implying inexperience. He worried that the diminutive "Jack" was unfitting for the statesmanlike image which he sought to project.

Immediately following the 1960 Democratic Convention, Robert Kennedy fired out a memo to all persons who represented or spoke for his brother. He asked them to refer to JFK in the future as "Senator" Kennedy instead of "Jack." Even Kennedy's top aide, Theodore "Ted" Sorensen felt the pressure of formality:

> It took me a few years to address him as "Jack" instead of "Senator," and we agreed in 1957 that the decorum befitting a national political aspirant required that I return to calling him "Senator" in the presence of others. But "Jack" was still the accepted salutation in private until January 20, 1961.

"Mr. President" insisted on being dealt with formally, while he reserved the right to deal formally or informally with anyone as he pleased. Apparently, this precedent of style was lost on "Jimmy" Carter.

*

"Call up that Jack Kennedy," said Senate Foreign Relations Committee Chairman J. William Fulbright to his assistant in order to have a quorum for a committee meeting. "All he does is sit there at the end of the table — if you ever get him here. And when he does sit down there, he sits there autographing pictures of himself." Senator Fulbright aptly described Senator Kennedy's attitude toward meetings. He found them too boring, too time consuming with too many discussions and not enough action. His preferred style of governing was anti-bureaucratic and pro-central control. In an emergency, such as the Cuban Missile Crisis, he called upon an ad hoc committee rather than relying on the established, phlegmatic, bureaucratic government.

Where did Kennedy acquire his distaste for bureaucracies? Perhaps his father's free-enterprising style and subsequent success influenced him. Possibly he acquired his taste for quick decisions and fast action as a PT-109 captain. In a discussion with Theodore White at the 1960 Democratic Convention in Los Angeles, a Kennedy aide suggested that Kennedy's new generation of war veterans learned about circumventing bureaucracies in World War II.

"You know, I used to think during the war that people who stayed home in their jobs were getting ahead of us," the aide told White. The aide continued:

> There we were overseas, losing all those years. And there they were at home getting ahead. Now I feel sorry for the older men. I think we learned something during the war about how to do things; we learned how to work in a way the generals didn't understand. They'd tell us what to do, but then we had to go out and organize the thing — cut the red tape, get the stuff there on time, no matter how, throw away the rule book. We learned to work together without any fussing. The other day when they tried to change the rules here against us, nobody got frantic or excited. Larry (O'Brien) just said to Kenny (O'Donnell), "I think we ought to get our fellows on the rules committee to work on it," and Kenny said, "I guess your right. I'll round them up and give them the word." And that was it. No conferences or planning. I think we learned to work that way during the way, and I feel sorry for the older fellows who never learned.

America's first television president wanted quick action when he arrived at the White House. He promised in his campaign speeches to get America moving again, and he delivered by dismantling bureaucratic procedure whenever possible.

Sorensen described Kennedy's communication style:

> He abandoned the practice of the Cabinet's and the National Security Council's making group decisions like corporate boards of directors. He abolished the practice of White House staff meetings and weekly Cabinet meetings. He abolished the pyramid structure of the White House staff, the Assistant President — Sherman-Adams-type job, the Staff Secretary, the Cabinet Secretary, the NSC Planning Board and the Operations Coordinating Board, which imposed, in his view, needless paperwork and machinery between the president and his responsible officers. He abolished several dozen interdepartmental committees which specialized in group recommendations on outmoded problems. He paid little attention to organization charts and chains of command which diluted and distributed his authority. He was not interested in unanimous committee recommendations which stifled alternatives to find the lowest common denominator of compromise.

The State Department turned out to be a huge bureaucracy (also known as the "permanent government") with which Kennedy was always at odds and which he could not dismantle. "I can hire fewer than one hundred thirty. Presidents come and go but those bastards stay there forever," the president complained about State. Kennedy referred to the State Department as "a bowl of jelly" because of its propensity for spineless decisions and bureaucratic inaction.

"I have discovered finally that the best way to deal with State is to send over memos," Kennedy told Arthur Schlesinger. "They can forget phone conversations, but a memorandum is something which, by their system, has to be answered. So let's put as many things as possible in memoranda from now on."

Kennedy used his staff as watchdogs over the State Department. Often the staff would find out that State was not following the orders it was instructed to carry out. The president would be informed of this and would call State to remind it of its responsibilities. As the press learned of Kennedy's style of dealing with the State Department, they accused the White House of "meddling" in State's affairs. During the Berlin Crisis Schlesinger wondered aloud to the president whether they should ask the sensitive State Department to rewrite a white paper on Berlin. Kennedy answered that State "... ought to read the Constitution over there and find out who was responsible for foreign affairs and whose government it was anyway."

The president's bureaucratic problem existed not only at the State Department; he soon found another one in the Navy. In 1963, a Venezuelan freighter was hijacked by some communists. After learning that nothing was being done to help Caracas with the problem, the president phoned the Secretary of the Navy to ask why planes were not sent out to find the ship. The secretary explained that it was not his responsibility; he could only act if requested to do so by the Joint Chiefs of Staff. Later that week Venezuelan President Betancourt visited the White House for a great military reception had been planned, but unfortunately, cancelled because of a rainstorm. When Kennedy gazed out his window an hour later and saw a group of rain drenched soldiers still standing in formation, he called his military aide, General Clifton, to ask why they were still there. He replied that he was awaiting orders from the proper military channels. Kennedy — as Commander-In-Chief — circumvented the ridiculous bureaucracy and ordered Clifton to send the soldiers home immediately. To

Schlesinger, the president complained, "You can see why the Navy has been unable to locate that Venezuelan freighter."

In his 1965 book, Schlesinger mentioned that when he first joined Kennedy's staff as a writer, he found the relationship between the other aides relatively tranquil. He attributed this to the paucity of staff meetings. Staff meetings allowed the opportunity for the expression of opposing views which could then create open disagreements. Kennedy's style of calling infrequent meetings enabled him to meet with and read reports from his individual staff members. To Kennedy, the function of staff members was to provide information based on their individual specialities without first consulting with others to build a consensus opinion.

White House aide Fred Dutton once complained about the president:

> He was hard to work for because he did not lead you to anything. You had to be a self-starter. Before Cabinet meetings I'd ask him what he wanted discussed. "You think of something" he said. He hated meetings. He was bored by them. And so we'd have them with decreasing frequency. If you were working for him, it was up to you to get the ball in the air. If he didn't like it, he'd say, "What a goddamn idea that is!"

Rather than conducting Cabinet meetings on a regular basis, Kennedy instead requested weekly reports from his cabinet members. The president once told John Sharon, "Cabinet meetings are simply useless. Why should the Postmaster General sit there and listen to a discussion of the problems of Laos?"

Kennedy Kinesics

Kinesics is the scientific name for the study of body

language or body communication. In kinesics, the use of facial expressions and body movements or gestures can reinforce or impede a spoken message. Kennedy's kinesics and physical appearance created an attractive media image.

Why did Kennedy's appearance create so much attention? The three presidents prior to him, Roosevelt, Truman, and Eisenhower, were balding older men. In comparison to them, Kennedy's youth and svelt good looks made him seem even more attractive than he was. When traveling in a motorcade, Kennedy's presence would turn normally calm women into "Jumpers." His charisma so excited the women lined along the streets that they would jump and leap up and down hoping to get a longer look at the "TV handsome" candidate.

Kennedy's copper-brown thick hair caused such a national sensation that he received letters about it, had its length exaggerated in editorial cartoons, and even read reports about it in *The New York Times*. The hair served as a symbol of virility and youth.

One time when presidential aide McGeorge Bundy visited the president, he saw first hand the attention Kennedy paid to his coiffure:

> Feldman and I dropped in on him in the Oval Office when he was having one of his pretty girls rubbing some goo on his hair, some perfect prescription that somebody had recommended for healthy hair. I said I didn't think this kind of thing was sufficiently dignified for the Oval Office. He looked around at Mike and me, both of us without much hair, and said, "Well, I'm not sure you two plan your hair very well."
>
> He was just terrible about his hair. He had that damn comb in his pocket and went through that hair at least fifty times a day. I don't know what he would have done if he lost his hair.

Evelyn Lincoln recalled the many letters which her boss received regarding his hair. "They were always asking why he didn't get a haircut or buy a brush or use some pomade." One letter even asked, "Why don't you have a hair style of your own instead of copying Mamie Eisenhower?"

Kennedy's appearance and activities provided a wealth of material for editorial cartoonists. When Senator Kennedy entered the Wisconsin primary, his family and in-laws campaigned by barnstorming throughout the state. They appeared at teas, ladies' clubs, supermarkets, and were seen on television. Lincoln observed that the newspapers all over the state were filled with cartoons portraying the family. "The senator enjoyed these cartoons, and I wrote many letters to political cartoonists asking if the senator could have the originals for his parents, for Eunice, or for himself. I covered the wall of his office with these cartoons, and he took a great deal of pride in showing them to visitors."

On May 9, 1963, the president greeted a group of editorial cartoonists in the Flower Garden at the White House. During his speech he facetiously admonished them for exaggerating his thick, bushy hair. "I am glad to have you here, and am going to examine what you have done to us with some concern. You see, the hair is much less than you have it!"

Soon after Senator Kennedy declared himself a candidate for president, *The New York Times* on January 12, 1960 printed a report entitled, "Kennedy's Unruly Hair Gets Political Training." The report asked, "Has Senator John F. Kennedy finally tamed that unruly shock of hair, in the hope of improving his candidacy for the Presidency?" The article went on to speculate that it appeared that Kennedy's barber had finally figured out a way to control his "boyish-looking forelock." "Some of Mr. Kennedy's friends say he hopes to make himself appear more mature. Aides in his Senate office refused to discuss the matter. At his campaign headquarters here (Washington, D.C.) Pierre Salinger, press assistant, told a reporter: 'I think you're wrong. I haven't noticed any change in his hair-do at all.'"

*

Our first TV president was always concerned about his appearance, particularly his face. "Physical characteristics exert a profound influence over one's associates," wrote Frances Cooke Macgregor in *Transformation and Identity.* "The fact that physically attractive people elicit favorable responses is obvious to anyone who has observed his fellow men. Physical qualities pleasing to see or touch are definitely assets . . . in making their possessors more popular . . . ." Kennedy understood this all too well.

Kennedy was known for his year-round tan. The tan was maintained by his habit of sailing, his trips to his parents' home in Palm Beach, and by the use of a sunlamp during the colder months. As another sign of his vanity, Kennedy, prior to the Inauguration, made a dental appointment to get his teeth cleaned.

"My God! Look at that fat face," Kennedy complained to his secretary as he looked in a mirror and pulled at his cheeks. "If I don't lose five pounds this week I might have to call of the Inauguration." It was not always clear whether his face became fuller-looking because of overeating or because of an adrenal insufficiency. It is now known that the cortisone derivative he took to combat this ailment often made his face appear fuller. "Vain as always," said Benjamin Bradlee of Kennedy, "it bugged him if he appeared a little jowly at press conferences . . . ."

As a freshman senator, Kennedy did not pay complete attention to his style of dressing. Mrs. Lincoln remembered his disheveled appearance at the swearing-in ceremony as senator. ". . . I noticed him trying to button his coat to hide his necktie, which was hanging down far below his belt." He continued to dress haphazardly until after his marriage to Jacqueline. "It was so odd to me the way he grew in stages," his secretary said. "From a fumbling person who couldn't tie his own tie, and it was always too long, to an immaculate dresser. Jackie was so immaculate and maybe it rubbed off on him." Kennedy subsequently became so confident and adept in dressing properly that he once jokingly advised his friend, Charles Spalding, "Your suit doesn't make a statement."

Kennedy was also concerned about the appearance of photographs taken of him. He resented photographers who attempted to take a picture of him wiping sweat from his brow during a speech. Because of his aversion to wearing any hats offered to him on the campaign trail, he would either refuse gracefully to try it on or would put it on and take it off so quickly that photographers could not get a picture.

During his senate years he would sometimes come across pictures of himself in some Massachusetts newspapers that were taken during his congressional days. Since the pictures showed him as thin and sickly looking, he would have his administrative assistant, Ted Reardon, reissue some more current photographs to the papers. This president understood fully the impact of photos and photo opportunities in politics. While campaigning for president, he made a special effort to pose with all state and local politicians and dignitaries in order to enhance their status.

*

As any public speaker knows, gestures play an important role in speech making. With head tilted back slightly, chin jutting forward, left hand in suit pocket, and right hand and forefinger chopping the air up and down to emphasize points, Kennedy would use his "trademark" limited number of gestures during a speech. Rose Kennedy felt that her son learned his staccato gestures and fast speaking style from her.

Kennedy strove to maintain a sense of dignity, class, and self-controlled "cool" reserve while speaking. By this means he would differentiate himself from some typical "hot" (in the Marshall McLuhan sense of the word) politicians' speaking style. For example, he would never be seen waving both arms above his head. "If I have to hold both hands above my head to be president," he told a friend, "I'm not going to be president."

Over a period of time, Evelyn Lincoln learned to interpret Kennedy's gestures around the office:

> You could tell when things were annoying him. He'd tap his fingers of his right hand if he was talking to someone. If he was having a meeting and he was sitting on his rocker, he would be swinging his right foot if things weren't going well. And if he was really annoyed, his left eye would get a little askew and sort of droop a little, as if there was an irritation behind it. Then I would know something was really wrong. My job was to move in anytime I saw any sign of this. I could tell him there was a phone call for him so he could break away for a while. I had to anticipate what he was going to do in order to relieve his feelings. It's a little bit of an art.

Apparently Kennedy kinesics were learned mostly from his mother, Rose. Mrs. Kennedy believed that "... attention to details, even the minor gestures that are part of human communication, is important in all human relationships."

Speech Writing Style

The Kennedy style of speech writing was actually a combination of his and Theodore Sorensen's writing style. Of course, many other writers contributed to Kennedy's speeches, but Sorensen played the principle role.

Kennedy's speeches were never longer than twenty to thirty minutes in duration. They contained numerous fact and statistics and often many quotations from famous people. *Bartlett's Quotations* served as his primary resource for quotations along with Agar's *The Price of Union*.

In his opening statement in the first Kennedy-Nixon Debate, Kennedy began, "In the election of 1860, Abraham Lincoln said the question was whether this nation could exist half-slave or half-free . . . ." Kennedy would also quote people from the field of literature. During his birthday dinner remarks at the Boston (Mass.) Armory, he said the following:

> I want to also thank Mr. Frost for saying an Irish poem over us. He spoke very highly of Harvard, but I do think it appropriate to reveal that on the morning after the Inaugural when he came to the White House, he said, "You're something of Irish and I suppose something of Harvard. My advice to you as president is to be Irish." So we're going to do the best we can.

"Our chief criterion was always audience comprehension and comfort," said Sorensen describing the speech writing style. Speeches were written not to be pleasing to the eye, but to sound appealing to the ear. The essence of the style, Sorensen continued, included: "(1) short speeches, short clauses and short words, wherever possible; (2) a series of points or propositions in numbered or logical sequence, wherever appropriate; and (3) the construction of sentences, phrases and paragraphs in such a manner as to simplify, clarify, and emphasize."

While speaking in a foreign land, Kennedy would often personalize his speech by saying a few words in the country's native language. In this way, he showed his interest in the audience by going to the trouble of learning a few foreign words. Arriving at the Royal Canadian Air Force Uplands Airport in Ottawa on May 16, 1961, the president gave his first speech out of the country and spoke partly in French to the appreciative audience. His translated French said: "This is my first trip away from the United States since I succeeded to the Presidency. It is fitting that I should come here to Canada, the oldest of our neighbors and among the closest of our friends." His most famous speech abroad, however, was to the West Germans around the time of the Berlin Crisis. In that speech he reassured the German people and affirmed, in their own language, "We are all Berliners": "All free men, wherever they may live, are citizens of Berlin, and therefore as a free man, I take pride in the words Ich bin ein Berliner!"

Kennedy had a great sense of humor; his speeches reflected his humorous style. He preferred to use humor at the beginning of his speeches; it was rarely used in the body of a drafted speech. "(Kennedy) believed topical, tasteful, pertinent, pointed humor at the beginning of his remarks to be a major means of establishing audience rapport," recalled Sorensen. Kennedy's use of humor is discussed in greater detail in the next chapter.

Cultural Style

At his presidential inauguration, Kennedy signaled a cultural revival by having Robert Frost read a poem during the opening ceremonies. The president believed that his official recognition of the arts in America would instill a greater appreciation of culture by all Americans.

From the inaugural platform, Frost began to read a poem he had written for the occasion:

Summoning artists to participate
In the august occasions of the state
Seems something artists ought to celebrate.

At this point the poet stopped and stated, "I'm not having a good light here at all. I can't see in this light." As the bright sun and snow blinded him, Lyndon Johnson used his hat to shade the light from the poem, but to no avail. Frost, however, continued and recited one of his poems from memory. The original poem he wrote concluded as follows:

> It makes the prophet in us all presage
> The glory of a next Augustan age
> Of a power leading from its strength and pride,
> Of young ambition eager to be tried,
> Firm in our free beliefs without dismay,
> In any game the nations want to play.
> A golden age of poetry and power
> Of which this noonday's the beginning hour.

Frost was honored by the invitation to the Inaugural ceremony and knew what it meant to his fellow artists and writers. "If you can bear at your age the honor of being made president of the United States, I ought to be able at my age to bear the honor of taking some part in your Inauguration," replied Frost in his acceptance letter to Kennedy. "I may not be equal to it but I can accept it for my cause — the arts, poetry, now for the first time taken into the affairs of statesmen." Kennedy proved his cultural interest by not only asking Frost to speak, but by inviting over fifty other writers, composers, and painters to the ceremony. Arthur Schlesinger noted that the president's attention paid to culture seemed ". . . to prefigure a new Augustan age of poetry and power."

How or why did Kennedy acquire an interest in the arts? According to Rose Kennedy, it was Jacqueline who ". . . developed (the president's) interests in art, music, and poetry - especially poetry, in which he had had only a mild interest before." Months after Kennedy had invited Pablo Casals to perform at the White House, he continued to receive praise about helping the cause of classical music. Jackie would tease the president about this and joked, "The only music he really appreciates is 'Hail to the Chief.' "

The president's wife had an exquisite (and expensive) taste for clothes and a preference for French culture. She received continuous praise from the media, and many American women copied her style of dress. Long evening gowns, pill box hats, and white gloves became popular during her reign as First Lady.

Jacqueline Kennedy also had a gift for writing. A month after her marriage to Kennedy, she wrote a laudatory poem about him, a poem which helped to gain her the affection and respect of the Kennedy clan. The poem, written in October of 1953, displayed the cultural sensibilities which encouraged Jack Kennedy's appreciation of the arts.

*

Two memorable cultural events in Washington D.C. were the performance of Pablo Casals and a dinner honoring American Nobel Prize winners. Kennedy paid tribute to the cellist, Pablo Casals, by inviting him to give a concert at the White House on the evening of November 13, 1961. "We feel that your performance as one of the world's greatest artists would lend distinction to the entertainment of our invited guests," wrote the president to Casals. On another occasion, Kennedy invited forty-nine Nobel Prize winners to the White House to honor their achievements. Also attending the event were one hundred and twenty-four scientists, writers, editors, and educators. Kennedy devoted so much time to this entertaining that he once joked to a group of intellectuals that the White House was ". . . becoming a sort of eating place for artists. But *they* never ask *us* out."

*

On December 18, 1962, *Look* magazine published an article written by the president entitled "The Arts in America." In it he outlined his feelings on the role of culture in America.

He mentioned that Americans have neglected the arts. "Too often in the past, we have thought of the artist as an idler and dilettante and of the lover of arts as somehow sissy or effete. We have done both an injustice." Throughout the article, he preached that the pursuit of the arts was worthwhile. The federal government, he believed, should serve as "an example and teacher" of the arts by promoting them.

"I have called for a higher degree of physical fitness in our nation," wrote the president. "It is only natural that I should call, as well, for the kind of intellectual and spiritual fitness which underlie the flowering of the arts."

Kennedy hoped that visitors and tourists to the nation's capital would be so inspired by the myraid of museums and monuments that they would then create and explore the arts in their own communities. Symphony orchestras, local repertory theaters, and opera and ballet groups were frequently invited to Washington D.C. to perform and serve as a signal to the country. Today the John F. Kennedy Center for the Performing Arts pays tribute to these artists.

*

Three further steps the president took to promote the arts were the creation of the Presidential Medal of Freedom, the

Advisory Council on the Arts, and the Fine Arts Committee. "A nation reveals itself not only by the men it produces but also by the men it honors," explained the president as he proclaimed the Medal of Freedom Awards as a yearly event. Kennedy took a personal interest in the award; he labored over its design and, although a committee was enlisted to make recommendations for honorees, he suggested some of his own. Ironically, a Presidential Medal of Freedom was awarded posthumously to Kennedy by President Johnson on December 6, 1963.

By executive order, Kennedy established the Advisory Council on the Arts. "Obviously government can at best play only a marginal role in our cultural affairs," Kennedy advised August Heckscher, his Special Consultant on the Arts. "But I would like to think that it is making its fullest contribution in this role."

Through presidential approval, Jackie Kennedy appointed a Fine Arts Committee to oversee the restoration of the White House. She believed that the White House should be attended to like a museum, rather than just being a temporary house for a president. With her curator and secretary, Jackie searched every room in the White House and discovered priceless relics worthy of restoration. Both President and Mrs. Kennedy strove earnestly to turn Washington D.C. into a beacon of American culture.

Kennedy's style of governing promoted culture through presidential recognition of the arts. By conducting honorary dinners and Medal of Freedom Award presentations, the president received heavy media coverage for these ceremonies. In effect, Kennedy employed the presidency to endorse the arts and thereby to legitimize them for all Americans.

Adversary Democrats

In his struggle for the presidency in 1960, Kennedy had to battle two influential, adversary Democrats, President Harry Truman and Eleanor Roosevelt. Kennedy revealed a facet of his communication style in the manner he handled the verbal onslaught from them.

Kennedy abided by a special belief about political relationships. "In politics you don't have friends. You have allies," he once said. He was fond of a book entitled, *The Great Game of Politics*, by Frank Kent. The author wrote about the importance of teamwork and allies and especially the significance of handshakes after the political "games."

Jaqueline Kennedy was a novice at this game of politics. Sometimes Kennedy would tell her about a politician that was fighting him on some issue. Jackie presumed that she should dislike the politician in question because of his adverse actions aimed at her husband.

"Are you saying nice things about (whomever)? I've been hating him for three weeks," Jackie would say to Kennedy after he praised a fellow he previously criticized. Kennedy would explain, "No, no, that was three weeks ago. Now he has done (something helpful)." In politics, he believed that one should never get into a disagreement which might obviate reconciliation at a later date. Today's foe could always be tomorrow's friend.

*

Perhaps Truman's quarrel with Kennedy began when the latter's father, Ambassador Joseph Kennedy Sr. had a falling out with President Roosevelt during the 1940's, and let Truman know about it. The ambassador was a pacifist prior to Japan's attack on Pearl Harbor and felt that World War II was Europe's war. Campaigning in Massachusetts for

President Roosevelt's fourth term of office, Truman encountered the ambassador's rage: "Harry, what are you doing campaigning for that crippled son of a bitch that killed my son Joe?"

"If you say another word about Roosevelt, I'm going to throw you out that window," Truman answered. Despite the argument, Kennedy Sr. assured Truman, through channels, that they were still friends and he donated $5000 to the Democratic party. Nonetheless, Truman was unsure about the ambassador and knew that many believed that should his son John someday aspire for the presidency, he would merely be a puppet of his domineering father.

John Kennedy respected Truman. As senator, Kennedy organized a fund-raising project for the Truman Library. Mrs. Lincoln found his effort in this surprising since he had worked against some of President Truman's policies when he was a congressman.

On January 10, 1960, Kennedy and Truman met to discuss the upcoming race for president. "The present administration has put this country in a terrible condition and it is vitally important that we have a change in power," Truman said to the senator. After the meeting, Kennedy told his secretary, "I was unable to find out which candidate he is going to back in 1960, but he did say that he would never do anything to hurt me."

Untrue to his promise, Truman on July 2, 1960 said on television that he would not participate in or attend a Democratic convention that had been "prearranged" by Kennedy. In his damaging statement, Truman charged that Kennedy was far too young and inexperienced and named some other candidates which he preferred. He also stated that Kennedy "... wasn't even dry behind the ears." Not only was the speech harmful to Kennedy's campaign, but Truman had attacked the senator on his own medium, television.

Phoning his office when he heard about the telecast, Kennedy complained, "Imagine making a statement like that on the eve of the convention."

The question now was: How could the campaign be salvaged from the broadside blasts of the influential Truman? Kennedy decided to deploy television to shoot down the former president's allegations. He first contacted the TV networks and requested equal time under Section 315 of the Communications Act. The networks informed him that the law did not apply since Truman was not seeking political office.

At the suggestion of NBC, Kennedy called a press conference for July 4. NBC agreed to cover the conference live and offered the other declared candidates — Lyndon Johnson and Stuart Symington — the same opportunity for free air time. Both declined. When Bob Kinter of NBC informed Johnson of Kennedy's press conference, Johnson naively said, "Terrific — he'll destroy himself." Campaign Manager Robert Kennedy asked Kinter to call Frank Stanton at CBS to persuade the station to televise the event. The Kennedy team was not pleased with CBS because of Stanton's close relationship with Johnson. They felt that Stanton was Johnson's "media errand boy." As he had feared, Kennedy did not see CBS at the beginning of his press conference. In fact, the network did not arrive until the conference was half over.

At the press conference, Kennedy deftly refuted every one of Truman's charges. In response to the claim that the convention was prearranged, the candidate answered that the majority of his votes came from the open primary system; he had won all seven which he had entered. Neither Johnson or Symington chose to participate in the primaries. With respect to the youth issue, he asserted that his fourteen years as an elected public servant was more time served than had

Woodrow Wilson, Franklin Roosevelt, and Harry Truman at the time that they had become president. Kennedy also insisted that he was older than the following men at significant times in their lives: George Washington as commander of the Continental Army; Thomas Jefferson as writer of the Declaration of Independence; and Christopher Columbus as discoverer of America. The press conference was a perfect example of the communication style that he strove for and discussed in his *Profiles In Courage:* "grace under pressure." He closed the televised event by saying, "I do not intend to step aside at anyone's request."

True to his political philosophy, Kennedy did not harbor a grudge against Truman. Immediately following his Democratic Convention victory, he phoned the former president and obtained his promise to support him during the upcoming campaign against the Republican victor. After becoming president, Kennedy invited and met with Truman at the White House; it was Truman's first visit there since he had left office in 1953. On May 8, 1961, Truman celebrated his 77th birthday with more than 200 friends at the Muehlebach Hotel in Kansas City, Missouri. When Kennedy called to wish him a happy birthday, Truman replied, "You are just as kind as you can be, and I more than appreciate it. You're better to me than I deserve."

*

Eleanor Roosevelt, the wife of Franklin Delano Roosevelt, like Truman, had misgivings about a Kennedy presidency. Mrs. Roosevelt was also suspicious of Kennedy's father and religion. When she protested on television that Kennedy Sr. spent too much money on his son's presidential campaign, the candidate demanded a retraction. She refused saying ". . . her information came largely from remarks made by people in many places."

When the Democratic Convention convened on July 11, 1960, Mrs. Roosevelt wanted Kennedy to display "unselfishness and courage" by seeking only the vice presidency. In that position, she thought that he would have "the opportunity to grow and learn." However, after becoming the Democratic nominee, Kennedy traveled to Hyde Park for a unity meeting and won Mrs. Roosevelt's support.

How would President Kennedy treat Mrs. Roosevelt, after having taken her verbal abuse prior to the Democratic Convention? He appointed her Chairwoman of the President's Commission on the Status of Women. The commission was established to make reports to the president, suggesting how to assist women seeking employment and overcoming discrimination. It also studied whether women were ". . . receiving compensation in accordance with the service they render . . . ." The president also agreed to be interviewed by Mrs. Roosevelt, on April 22, 1962, for a show on National Educational Television to discuss the commission that she headed and the role of women in America. Because of Kennedy's communication style of bearing no grudges, Mrs. Roosevelt, once a great foe of his, became a great friend.

Electronic Hardball

In his battle with the steel companies in April of 1962, President Kennedy's communication style enabled him to achieve victory. A careful analysis showed that Kennedy's media skills played a role in persuading the steel companies to renege on their $6 a ton price increase. Magnanimous in victory, the president took careful steps to regain a harmonious relationship with the steel companies.

On September 6, 1961, Kennedy wrote a letter to the

presidents of America's largest steel companies, asking them not to raise the price of steel in order to prevent any inflationary rise of consumer goods. In exchange for their price restraint, Kennedy and Labor Secretary Arthur Goldberg worked closely in negotiations between the steel union and the steel companies to help keep wages down.

Roger Blough, chairman of the United States Steel Corporation and chairman of the Business Advisory Council, was an active participant in all the discussions. When a new contract was due for the United Steel Workers in June of 1962, Kennedy's goal was to convince them to accept a noninflationary contract so that the steel companies would have no reason to raise the price of steel. Temporary success was achieved when the steel workers agreed to take no wage increase, save for a ten-cent-an-hour increase in fringe benefits.

All was well until Roger Blough phoned the White House to request a meeting with the president on April 10. Since Kennedy had met with Blough frequently during the previous months, he anticipated no crisis. Practicing his friendly proxemics, Kennedy with a handshake and smile welcomed Blough into his office and offered the couch to his guest while he sat in his rocking chair. Proxemics, a term coined by Dr. Edward T. Hall, is the study of social and personal space and man's perception of it. The president established an open, equal relationship with Blough by virtue of the seating arrangements. Had Kennedy sat behind his desk — the superior power spot in any office — with Blough before him in a chair, it could be assumed the president wanted to keep a less friendly relationship with him.

The cordial rapport soon ended, however. Blough handed Kennedy a four-page press release — given previously to the press that day — that announced the United States Steel Corporation was raising the steel price from $170 to $176 a ton. It was a daring double-cross. "I think you're making a mistake," Kennedy warned the chairman.

The first TV president was furious. To Benjamin Bradlee, he fumed, "Is this the way the private enterprise system is really suppose to work? When U.S. Steels says 'Go,' the boys go? How could they all raise their prices almost to a penny within six hours of each other?" Kennedy felt the price raise was unjustified because the steelworkers maintained their current wages. What really hurt Kennedy was the fact that he had helped to convince the steelworkers to hold the line on wage increases, while fully expecting Blough to do the same with the price of steel.

At a meeting with his aides, he said, "My father always told me that all steel men were sons-of-bitches, but I never realized till now how right he was." It was time to strike back. It was time for electronic hardball.

Kennedy chose to launch a campaign against the steel companies with an opening statement at his live televised News Conference on April 11. He also ordered three Cabinet officers — McNamara, Hodges, and Dillon, to hold press conferences and explain how the price increase would hurt the average American.

"Simultaneous and identical actions of United States Steel and other leading steel corporations increasing steel prices by some $6 a ton constitute a wholly unjustifiable and irresponsible defiance of the public interest," began Kennedy at the press conference. "Some time ago I asked each American to consider what he would do for his country and I asked the steel companies. In the last 24 hours we had their answer."

Kennedy took advantage of television to turn public opinion against the steel companies. The first telegrams that he received after the press conference showed that public opinion was 2.5 to 1 in the president's favor.

Kennedy soon took some other strong measures, but he voiced his argument first on his favorite medium, TV. After being attacked publically on television, threatened with anti-trust suits, served subpoenas by the Justice Department for documents relating to a planned grand jury investigation of the price increase, and threatened by the loss of multimillion dollar government contracts, the major steel companies returned the price of steel to its previous cost. All this was accomplished in just 72 hours.

It was now a time for healing. True to his communication style, Kennedy called for a truce between the government and the steel companies. Asked whether he would now hold an anti-business attitude, Kennedy replied, "No, no, we're not going to do that. They're our partners — unwilling partners. But we're in this together. I want business to do well. If they don't, we don't."

After the steel crisis, Roger Blough came to the White House to confer with the president. An air of formality filled the Oval Office. Kennedy sat behind his desk after leading the chairman to a chair beside the desk. After sober discussions, they both agreed to work together as partners. As a peace gesture, Kennedy later sent a congratulatory letter to Roger Blough, who was being honored by Yale University. Also, on April 30, 1962, Kennedy delivered a speech before the United States Chamber of Commerce praising it on its 50th anniversary.

Every president faces conflicts during his term in office. Kennedy's communication style and skillful use of the media, more often than not, helped him to overcome adversity.

NOTES

75
Television shifted people's attention: Tony Schwartz, *Media: The Second God* (Garden City, New York: Anchor Books, 1983), p. 114.

75
"Mothers may still want": William Morris (ed.), *The American Dictionary of the English Language* (Boston: Houghton Mifflin Company, 1981), p. 1015.

75
". . . the fact remains that politics": Evelyn Lincoln, *My Twelve Years With John F. Kennedy* (New York: Bantam Books, Inc., 1965), p. 107.

76
Roosevelt grew-up as a nearsighted: Details of Theodore Roosevelt's health are in Samuel and Dorothy Rosenman, *Presidential Style* (New York: Harper & Row, Publishers, 1976), pp. 3f.

76
"If a mosquito bit Jack": Rose Kennedy, *Times To Remember* (Garden City, New York: Doubleday Company, Inc., 1974), p. 202.

77
"Mr. Kennedy who is usually hatless": Gene Brown (ed.), *The Kennedys — A New York Times Profile* (New York: Arno Press, 1980), p. 63.

77
"Now on those key jobs": Arthur M. Schlesinger Jr., *A Thousand Days* (New York: Fawcett Premier Books, 1965), p. 125.

78
"too ideological, too earnest": Ralph G. Martin, *A Hero For Our Time — An Intimate Story of the Kennedy Years* (New

York: Macmillan Publishing Company, 1983), p. 243.

78
"He's a very common man": Theodore H. White, *The Making Of The President 1960* (New York: Antheneum House, Inc., 1961) p. 67.

78
The New Frontier Administration: See Martin, p. 243.

78
Kennedy's Special Military Representative: See David Halberstam, *The Best and the Brightest* (New York: Random House, 1969), p. 163.

78
The communication style: Ibid., p. 21.

78
"my intellectual blood bank": Martin, p. 202.

78
"As their relationship grew stronger": Lincoln, p. 206.

79
"In a situation like that": Kenneth P. O'Donnell, David F. Powers, and Joe McCarthy, *"Johnny, We Hardly Knew Ye"* (Boston: Little, Brown and Company, 1970), p. 65.

79
"I am extremely sorry": Lincoln, p. 110.

80
As a matter of fact: Details of Kennedy's donating his salary to charities are in Theodore C. Sorensen, *Kennedy* (New York: Bantam Books, Inc., 1965), p. 21, and in Lincoln, p. 279.

81
acquaintances received: See Lincoln, p. 36.

81
Upon his return: Ibid., p. 60

81
Gold PT-109 boat tie clips: See Burton Hersh, *The*

Education of Edward Kennedy (New York: Dell Publishing Company, Inc., 1972), p. 190. See also Garry Wills, *The Kennedy Imprisonment* (Boston: Little, Brown and Company, 1981), p. 134.

81
The president gave cigarette lighters: See Lincoln, p. 291.

81
After Professor Archibald Cox: Ibid., p. 93.

81
Perhaps the most significant momento: Ibid., p. 276.

82
". . . there is simply no sense": Rose Kennedy, p. 471.

82
Mrs. Lincoln recalled: See Lincoln, pp. 2f.

82
"If you proved up to the task": Ibid., p. 2.

83
One day in the Oval Office: Ibid., p. 291.

83
"I simply cannot afford": Martin, p. 298.

83
President Kennedy received: See Jim Bishop, *A Day In The Life Of President Kennedy* (New York: Random House, Inc., 1964), p. 13.

84
Kennedy always studied: See Lincoln, p. 2.

84
"Buy her a good used television": Ibid., p. 16.

84
When Kennedy was growing up: See O'Donnell, Powers, and McCarthy, p. 44.

85
"Mrs. Lincoln, would you see that": Lincoln, p. 257.

85
"Listen you sons of bitches": Martin, p. 240.
86
Immediately following the 1960 Democratic Convention: See Lincoln, pp. 140f.
86
"It took me a few years": Sorensen, p. 32.
86
"Call up that Jack Kennedy": Martin, p. 104.
87
"You know, I used to think": White, *The Making Of The President 1960*, pp. 180f.
88
"He abandoned the practice of": Garry Wills, *The Kennedy Imprisonment* (Boston: Little, Brown and Company, 1981), pp. 166f.
88
"I can hire": Martin, p. 361.
88
"a bowl of jelly": Ibid., p. 360.
88
"I have discovered finally": Schlesinger, p. 400.
89
Kennedy used his staff as watchdogs: Ibid., pp. 391f.
89
". . . ought to read the Constitution": Ibid., p. 392.
90
"You can see why the Navy": Ibid., p. 629.
90
In his 1965 book: Ibid., pp. 195f.
90
"He was hard to work for": Martin, p. 304.
90
"Cabinet meetings": Schlesinger, p. 632.

91
"Feldman and I dropped in": Martin, p. 300.
91
"They were always asking": Lincoln, p. 97.
92
"The senator enjoyed these cartoons": Ibid., p. 111.
92
"I am glad to have you here": John F. Kennedy, *Public Papers of the Presidents of the United States (1963)* (Washington, D.C.: United States Government Printing Office, 1964), p. 381.
92
"Kennedy's Unruly Hair": Brown, p. 33.
93
"Physical characteristics": Frances Cooke Macgregor, *Transformation and Identity* (New York: Quadrangle/The New York Times Book Company, 1974), p. 35.
93
Kennedy was known: See Sorensen, p. 42.
93
As another sign: See Lincoln, p. 184.
93
"My God!": Ibid., pp. 183f.
93
"Vain as always": Benjamin C. Bradlee, *Conversations With Kennedy* (New York: Pocket Books, 1976), p. 70.
93
". . . I noticed him": Lincoln, p. 12.
94
"It was so odd to me": Martin, p. 103.
94
"Your suit doesn't make a statement": Ibid.
94
Kennedy was also concerned: See Sorensen, p. 31 and White,

The Making Of The President 1960, p. 288.
95
Rose Kennedy felt that: See Rose Kennedy, p. 316.
95
Kennedy strove to maintain: For an explanation of the terms "hot" and "cool," see Marshall McLuhan, *Understanding Media: The Extensions of Man* (New York: McGraw-Hill Book Company, 1964).
95
"If I have to hold": Sorensen, p. 203.
95
"You could tell when things": Martin, p. 301.
95
". . . attention to details": Rose Kennedy, p. 361.
95
The Kennedy style of speech writing: Details of Kennedy's speech writing style are in Sorensen, pp. 66ff.
96
"In the election of 1860": Sidney Kraus (ed.), *The Great Debates — Kennedy vs. Nixon, 1960* (Bloomington: Indiana University Press, 1962), p. 348.
96
"I want to thank Mr. Frost": John F. Kennedy, *Public Papers of the Presidents of the United States (1961)* (Washington, D.C.: United States Government Printing Office, 1962), p. 417.
96
"Our chief criterion": Sorensen, pp. 67f.
97
"This is my first trip": John F. Kennedy, *Public Papers (1961)*, p. 381.
97
"All free men": Rose Kennedy, p. 438.

97
"(Kennedy) believed": Sorensen, p. 70.
97
Summoning artists to participate: Schlesinger, p. 13.
98
"I'm not having a good light": Ibid.
98
"If you can bear": Ibid., p. 671.
98
". . . to prefigure a new Augustan age": Ibid.
98
". . . developed (the president's) interest in art": Rose Kennedy, p. 351.
99
"The only music": Hugh Sidey, *John F. Kennedy, President* (New York: Atheneum, 1964), p. 277.
99
"We feel that your performance": John F. Kennedy, *Public Papers (1961)*, p. 678.
100
". . . becoming a sort of eating place": Sorensen, p. 430.
100
"Too often in the past": John F. Kennedy, *Public Papers of the Presidents of the United States (1962)* (Washington, D.C.: United States Government Printing Office, 1963), p. 905.
100
"An example and teacher": Ibid., p. 906.
100
"I have called for a higher degree": Ibid., p. 905.
101
"A nation reveals itself": Sorensen, p. 430.
101
Ironically, a Presidential Medal of Freedom: See John F.

Kennedy, *Public Papers (1963)*, p. 903.
101
"Obviously government can at best": Schlesinger, p. 674.
102
"In politics you don't have friends": Rose Kennedy, p. 21.
102
"Are you saying nice things": Schlesinger, p. 101.
103
"Harry, what are you doing": Michael R. Beschloss, *Kennedy and Roosevelt — The Uneasy Alliance* (New York: W.W. Norton & Company, 1980), p. 259.
103
"The present administration": Lincoln, p. 100.
103
". . . wasn't even dry behind the ears": Ibid., p. 117.
104
"Imagine making a statement": Ibid.
104
"Terrific — he'll destroy himself": David Halberstam, *The Powers That Be* (New York: Dell Publishing Company, 1979), p. 459.
104
"media errand boy": Ibid., p. 458.
105
"grace under pressure": John F. Kennedy, *Profiles In Courage* (New York: Pocket Books, Inc., 1955), p. 1.
105
"I do not intend to step aside": Lincoln, p. 117.
105
"You are just as kind": John F. Kennedy, *Public Papers* (1961), p. 370.
105
". . . her information": Sorensen, p. 134.

106
"unselfishness and courage": Ibid., p. 175.
106
". . . receiving compensation in accordance": John F. Kennedy, *Public Papers (1962)*, p. 130.
106
The president also agreed: Text of Mrs. Roosevelt's interview is in John F. Kennedy, *Public Papers (1962)*, pp. 341ff.
107
Proxemics, a term coined by: Edward T. Hall, Ph.D., *The Hidden Dimension* (New York: Anchor Books, 1969), p. 1.
108
"I think you're making a mistake": Sidey, p. 293.
108
"Is this the way": Bradlee, pp. 77f.
108
"My father always told me": Sorensen, p. 504.
108
"Simultaneous and identical actions": John F. Kennedy, *Public Papers (1962)*, pp. 315ff.
108
The first telegrams: See Sidey, p. 299.
109
"No, no, we're not going to do that": Ibid., p. 303.

6

Kennedy Humor

"Mr. Nixon may be very experienced in kitchen debates, but so are a great many other married men I know!"

— Senator John F. Kennedy

President Kennedy was renowned for his use of humor. Speaking of the nation's capital, he once said, "Washington is a city of southern efficiency and northern charm." His humor was a natural part of his communication style.

When speaking in public, Kennedy understood that it is not simply "what you say" that counts; "how you say it" is also important. Audiences appreciate speakers who do not take themselves too seriously. Humor, particularly used by a speaker who aims it at himself, helps to bridge the gap that exists between a speaker and his audience. Simply stated, it is easier to persuade people to think your way if they like you as a person.

Kennedy can be compared to the national evening television news. The often-asked question today about the news is, "Is it news, or is it entertainment?" Well, it is actually both, but the entertainment helps to make news more appealing. Kennedy, like the news stations, had something to sell, that being himself and his political views. He attracted more media attention to himself because he was a handsome candidate with a good sense of humor.

Ted Sorensen kept a "humor folder" in his files for Kennedy. Campaigning throughout the country, Kennedy omitted humorous anecdotes from copies of his speeches that were distributed to the press. This usually stopped the quotes from reaching print so he could repeat them in other parts of the nation.

Within this chapter are selected quotations from Kennedy. They represent his characteristic humorous speaking style which made him a likable personality, both to friends and adversaries.

Early Years

While living in New York City, Kennedy at the age of twelve joined the boy scouts, which put a severe drain on his weekly allowance. Hopeful of getting an increase, young Kennedy composed the following artfully crafted "Chapter I" of a letter to his father wherein he requested a greater allowance (which was subsequently granted):

A Plea for a Raise
By Jack Kennedy
Dedicated to my Mr. J.P. Kennedy

Chapter I

My recent allowance is 40¢. This I used for areoplanes and other playthings of childhood but now I am a scout and I put away my childish things. Before I would spend 20¢ of my 40¢ allowance, and In five minutes I would have empty pockets and nothing to gain and 20¢ to lose. When I am a scout I have to buy canteens, haversacks, blankets searchliagts ponchos things that will last for years and I can always use it while I cant use a chocolate marshmellow sunday with vanilla ice cream and so I put in my plea for a raise of thirty cents for me to buy scout things and pay my own way around.

Finis

John Fitzgerald Francis Kennedy

*

The affluent, young John Kennedy was atypical of previous Boston Irish politicians. Many of the natives at first resented his candidacy. One evening, Kennedy appeared at a rally with dozens of other hopefuls who were running for state legislative seats. To Kennedy's annoyance, the chairman kept him waiting while he introduced speaker after speaker, praising each one as "a young fellow who came up the hard way." When finally introduced, Kennedy confessed:

"I seem to be the only person here tonight who didn't come up the hard way." (Laughter)

*

Plagued by back problems throughout his life, Kennedy once wrote to a friend about his first back surgery in 1944: "... I think the doc should have read just one more book before picking up the saw."

*

Kennedy met his wife, Jacqueline Lee Bouvier, when she interviewed him for the Inquiring Photographer column for *The Washington Times-Herald*. He later joked about how he first asked her out while attending a dinner party: "I leaned over the asparagus and asked her for a date."

The Senator

During World War II, Kennedy emerged a war hero by leading his surviving crewmates to safety after his PT-109 boat was rammed by the Amagiri, a Japanese destroyer. When a teenager in Ashland, Wisconsin asked him how he happened to be "a war hero," Kennedy answered: "It was involuntary. They sank my boat."

*

In the Democratic Convention in 1956, Senator Kennedy almost won the vice presidential nomination from Senator Estes Kefauver of Tennessee. This marked his first loss since entering public service in 1946. While he appeared to the public as taking the defeat as a "good sport," he confided to friends: "I feel like the Indian who had a lot of arrows stuck in him and when he was asked how he felt, said, 'It only hurts when I laugh.' "

*

In order not to alienate himself from even the poorest members of the Democratic party, Kennedy always downplayed his family's wealth. Once a newspaper story reported on Eunice Kennedy's wedding to Sargent Shriver. It stated that a Kennedy business associate had "smilingly acknowledged that its cost would run into six figures." After hearing this, JFK replied: "Now I know the story is a phony — no one in my father's office smiles."

*

The Kennedy family fortune constituted a great portion of the presidential campaign funds. Allegations from all quarters during the campaign claimed that the senator was trying to buy the election. During the West Virginia primary campaign, Hubert Humphrey complained, "I don't have any daddy who can pay the bills for me."

Appointed the role of Democratic jester for the Washington Gridiron Club Dinner in 1958, Kennedy chose to make light of his "rich boy" image. In a speech that he gave that night, Kennedy claimed to have just received a wire from his father, which said: "Dear Jack: Don't buy a single vote more than is necessary — I'll be damned if I'm going to pay for a landslide."

*

An issue that continually irked the senator was propagated by those who felt that he was too inexperienced for the office of president. Although he was younger than Nixon, and at the age of forty-three would be the youngest president ever elected, Kennedy along with Nixon shared the same number of years in public service: fourteen. To accentuate his vice presidential experience in the campaign, Nixon often recalled the time he shook his finger in Krushchev's face during their famous "kitchen debate" and boasted, "You may be ahead of us in rocket thrust but we are ahead of you in color television." During many of his speeches, the senator belittled Nixon's experience: "I will take my television in black and white. I want to be ahead in rocket thrust.... Mr. Nixon may be very experienced in kitchen debates, but so are a great many other married men I know."

*

Arriving late at a presidential campaign stop in Wilmington, Delaware, the golf loving Kennedy quipped: "Ladies and gentlemen, I want to apologize for keeping you waiting. I was not playing golf. We were over in New Jersey, campaigning."

*

Campaigning for president, Kennedy once spoke at a political rally in Lockport, New York. Mindful of the city's Republican mayor in the audience, Kennedy said: "I understand, Mr. Mayor, that you are a member of another active party in the United States. I hope you won't feel I am abusing the hospitality of the city if I say a few good words on behalf of the Democratic Party."

*

After The Great Debates in which Senator Kennedy met with Nixon four times, Kennedy made humorous remarks about the vice president's appearance. Because of the vice president's heavy beard, an advisor plastered his face with a pancake cosmetic called Max Factor's "Lazy Shave" prior to the televising of the first debate. The effect of all this had Nixon looking ghost-like, while Kennedy appeared more attractive due to his dark tan. Campaigning in New Mexico, Kennedy could not resist responding to Nixon's claim that he was a barefaced liar:

> Two days ago, the Republican candidate, Mr. Nixon, quoted me as having said that the Republicans had always opposed Social Security, and in that wonderful choice of words which distinguishes him as a great national leader, he asserted that this was a barefaced lie. Having seen him four times close up in this campaign, and made-up, I would not accuse Mr. Nixon of being barefaced — but I think the American people next Tuesday can determine who is telling the truth.

The President

Despite the anticipated charges of nepotism, Kennedy appointed his brother Robert as attorney general. Kennedy's press release about the appointment read as follows:

> In looking for an attorney general who must lead the fight for law enforcement, who must administer our laws without favor and with matchless integrity, I have turned to a man in whom I have found these qualities. I have every confidence that he will bring to his new position this same ability, this same energy, this same courage, this same independence of judgement, and this same integrity.

Speaking at a postinaugural dinner, the president confessed why he really hired his younger brother: "(To give) him a little experience before he goes out to practice law."

*

As president, Kennedy often received glowing introductions from local dignitaries. After being introduced repeatedly as "potentially the greatest president in the history of the United States," Kennedy once responded:

> I want to express my appreciation to the governor. Every time he introduces me as the potentially greatest president in the history of the United States, I always think perhaps he is overstating it one or two degrees. George Washington wasn't a bad president and I do want to say a word for Thomas Jefferson. But otherwise, I will accept the compliment.

*

Throughout her life, Rose Kennedy — the president's mother — collected autographs of famous people. She would normally ask leading personages to sign books which they had written or pictures taken of themselves. Even though the relationship between the United States and Russia during the Kennedy Administration was less than ideal, Mrs. Kennedy sent pictures taken of Premier Krushchev and her son during their sensitive Vienna meeting to Krushchev with a request for his autograph. Having received them back signed by the Russian leader, she sent them on to Kennedy, with a note requesting that he do the same so she could return the favor to Krushchev. Upon receipt of this unusual request, Kennedy fired a response to his mother:

Dear Mother:

    If you are going to contact the heads of state, it might be a good idea to consult me or the State Department first, as your gesture might lead to international complications.

                          Love,
                          Jack

To which she replied:

> Dear Jack:
>
> I am so glad you warned me about contacting the heads of state, as I was about to write Castro.
>
> > Love,
> > Mother

*

At the White House on April 29, 1962, Kennedy greeted Nobel Prize winners of the Western Hemisphere at a dinner reception in their honor. His introductory remarks began as follows:

> I want to welcome you to the White House. Mr. Lester Pearson informed me that a Canadian newspaperman said yesterday that this is the president's "Easter egghead roll on the White House lawn." I want to deny that! I want to tell you how welcome you are to the White House. I think this is the most extraordinary collection of talent, of human knowledge, that has been ever gathered together at the White House, with the possible exception of when Thomas Jefferson dined alone.

Press Conferences

After the Bay of Pigs fiasco in Cuba where a CIA sponsored invasion was thwarted, Kennedy accepted full responsibility for its failure. In response to a question about the invasion, Kennedy answered: "Victory has 100 fathers and defeat is an orphan."

*

Recalling a quote that was attributed to Kennedy — "My father always told me that steel men were sons-of-bitches...." — a reporter asked the following question:

Question: Mr. President, at the time of your controversy with the steel industry, you were quoted as making a rather harsh statement about businessmen. I am sure you know which statement I have in mind.
The President: Yes. You wouldn't want to identify it, would you? (Laughter)

*

Question: There's a feeling in some quarters, sir, that big business is using the stock market slump as a means of forcing you to come to terms with business. One reputable columnist, after talking to businessmen, obviously, reported this week their attitude is "now we have you where we want you." Have you seen any reflection of this attitude?
The President: I can't believe I'm where big business wants me. (Laughter)

*

In the following exchange, Kennedy displayed his self-effacing humor:

Question: Mr. President, going back to Berlin, I think the American people are confused by what they read and hear about Berlin. One day they read or they're told that American officials are encouraged by the outlook. Another day they read that they're not encouraged, that they're gloomy. One day we're going ahead, the next day we're going back. Mr. President, does the real situation fluctuate that much? As a one-time journalist who became president, how does it look to you?
The President: Well, a lot of journalists had bad luck. (Laughter)

*

Question: Mr. President, the Democratic platform in

which you ran for election promises to work for equal rights for women, including equal pay, and to wipe out job opportunity discriminations. Now you have made efforts on behalf of others. What have you done for the women, according to the promises of the platform?

The President: Well, I'm sure we haven't done enough. (Laughter) I must say I am a strong believer in equal pay for equal work, and I think we ought to do better than we're doing, and I'm glad you reminded me of it, Mrs. Craig. (Laughter)

*

Kennedy was instrumental in encouraging America's exploration of space, and he convinced congress to appropriate huge financial amounts to fulfill his dream. Due to the dangerous nature of early rocket travel, and the tendency for American ships to blow up on the launch pad, chimpanzees were used in the first test flights to test their reactions during space travel. Updating the press on that day's space flight, Kennedy read the following note: "This chimpanzee who is flying in space took off at 10:08. He reports that everything is perfect and working well." (Laughter)

*

During his presidency, Kennedy encouraged the drinking of milk. In response to concern expressed that milk was contaminated with radioactivity, Kennedy commented: "I was attempting to reassure . . . (there was no danger) . . . and also to seek if we can stimulate it by example. Mr. Salinger (press secretary) drank it this morning — (Laughter) — with no adverse effect."

*

Question: Mr. President, Congressman Alger of Texas today criticized Mr. Salinger as a "young and inexperienced White House publicity man" — (Laughter) — and questioned the advisability of having him visit the Soviet Union. I wonder if you have any comments.

The President: I know there are always some people who feel that Americans are always young and inexperienced, and foreigners are always able and tough negotiators. But I don't think the United States would have acquired its present position of leadership in the free world if that view were correct. Now he also, as I saw the press, said that Mr. Salinger's main job was to increase my standing in the Gallup poll. Having done that, he is now moving on — (Laughter) — to improve our communications.

*

The president, a former journalist, enjoyed teasing and joking with the press. An avid reader of newspapers, he closely followed the day's events:

Question: Mr. President, on a more local level, the *Washington Daily News* suggested today that since Colonel Glenn's achievements illustrate the ultimate in physical and scientific discipline, that all the school kids and all the surrounding schools in Maryland, Virginia and Washington be let out to welcome him here Monday. Would you go along with that suggestion?

The President: We always follow the *Washington Daily News* — (Laughter) — and I believe that that is being done.

*

Question: Mr. President, your brother Ted, recently on television said that after seeing the cares of office on you, that he wasn't sure he'd ever be interested in being the president. I wonder if you could tell us whether if you had it to do over again, you would work for the presidency, and whether you can recommend the job to others.

The President: Well, the answer is — to the first is "yes" and the second is "no." I don't recommend it to others — (Laughter) — at least for a while.

*

Always sensitive not to offend his colleagues in congress, Kennedy fielded the following question:

Question: Mr. President, you have said that you are in favor of a two-term limit to the office of presidency. How do you feel about former President Eisenhower's suggestion that the terms of congressman also be limited?

The President: It's the sort of proposal I may advance in a post-presidential period, but not right now. (Laughter)

*

Question: Mr. President, in the 1960 campaign, you used to say it was time for America to get moving again. Do you think it is moving, and if so, how and where? The reason I ask you the question, Mr. President, is that the Republican National Committee recently adopted a resolution saying you were pretty much a failure.

The President: I am sure it was passed unanimously. (Laughter)

*

Question: This being Valentine's Day, sir, do you think it might be a good idea if you would call Senator Strom Thurmond of South Carolina down to the White House for a heart-to-heart talk — (Laughter) — about the whole disagreement over the censorship of the military speeches and what he calls your defeatest foreign policy?

The President: Well, I think that meeting should probably be prepared at a lower level (Laughter).

NOTES

121
"Washington is a city": Arthur M. Schlesinger Jr., *A Thousand Days* (New York: Fawcett Premier Books, 1965), p. 618.

121
"humor folder": Theodore C. Sorensen, *Kennedy* (New York: Bantam Books, Inc., 1965), p. 70.

122
A Plea for a raise: Rose Kennedy, *Times To Remember* (Garden City, New York: Doubleday & Company, Inc., 1974), pp. 113f.

122
"a young fellow who came up the hard way": Kenneth P. O'Donnell, David F. Powers, and Joe McCarthy, *"Johnny, We Hardly Knew Ye"* (Boston: Little, Brown and Company, 1970), p. 59.

123
"I seem to be the only person": Ibid.

123
". . . I think the doc": Sorensen, p. 44.

123
"I leaned over the asparagus": Booton Herndon, *The Humor of JFK* (Greenwich, Conn.: Fawcett Publications, Inc., 1964), p. 26.

123
"It was involuntary": Ibid., p. 62.

123
"I feel like the Indian": Ibid., p. 27.

124
"smilingly acknowledged": Sorensen, p. 34.

124
"Now I know": Ibid.

124
"I don't have any daddy": Richard J. Whalen, *The Founding Father — The Story of Joseph P. Kennedy* (New York: The New American Library of World Literature, Inc., 1964), p. 452.
124
"Dear Jack": Ibid.
125
"You may be ahead of us": Sorensen, p. 206.
125
"I will take my television": Ibid.
125
"Ladies and gentlemen": Bill Adler, *More Kennedy Wit* (New York: Bantam Books, 1965), p. 29.
125
"I understand, Mr. Mayor": Ibid., p. 37.
126
"Two days ago": Herndon, p. 32.
126
"In looking for an attorney general": Evelyn Lincoln, *My Twelve Years With John F. Kennedy* (New York: Bantam Books, Inc., 1965), pp. 177f.
126
"(To give) him a little experience": Sorensen, p. 301.
127
"I want to express my appreciation": Herndon, pp. 71f.
127
"Dear Mother": Rose Kennedy, pp. 406f.
128
"I want to welcome you": John F. Kennedy, *Public Papers of the Presidents of the United States (1962)* (Washington, D.C.: United States Government Printing Office, 1963), p. 347.
128
"Victory has 100 fathers": John F. Kennedy, *Public Papers*

of the Presidents of the United States (1961) (Washington, D.C.: United States Government Printing Office, 1962), p. 312.

128
"My father always told me": Sorensen, p. 504.

129
Question: Mr. President, at the time: John F. Kennedy, *Public Papers* (1962), p. 379.

129
Question: There's a feeling: Adler, pp. 119f.

129
Question: Mr. President, going back to Berlin: John F. Kennedy, *Public Papers (1961)*, p. 660.

129
Question: Mr. President, the Democratic platform: Ibid., p. 709.

130
"This chimpanzee who is flying": Ibid., p. 761.

130
"I was attempting to reassure": John F. Kennedy, *Public Papers (1962)*, p. 63.

131
Question: Mr. President, Congressman Alger: Ibid., p. 97.

131
Question: Mr. President, on a more local level: Ibid., pp. 152f.

131
Question: Mr. President, your brother Ted: Ibid., p. 276.

132
Question: Mr. President, you have said: John F. Kennedy, *Public Papers of the Presidents of the United States (1963)* (Washington, D.C.: United States Government Printing Office, 1964), p. 95.

132
Question, Mr. President, in the 1960 campaign: Ibid., p. 571.

132
Question: This being Valentine's Day: John F. Kennedy, *Public Papers (1962)*, p. 136.

7

The White House Years

"It's almost impossible to write a story that they [the Kennedys] like. Even if a story is quite favorable to their side, they'll find one paragraph to quibble with."

— Benjamin C. Bradlee, Washington Bureau Chief of *Newsweek* during the Kennedy Administration

Charisma has been defined as "a rare quality or power attributed to those persons who have demonstrated an exceptional ability for leadership and for securing the devotion of large numbers of people." The Kennedy mystique and charisma charmed the country during the White House years. The image which he portrayed to the public and press reflected class, style, and excitement. Even today, whenever people are asked to name a charismatic leader, "President Kennedy" is a frequent response. Jacqueline Kennedy wanted those years to be remembered as the times of Camelot. One time, the president and his wife posed in formal party attire for the cover of the *New York Daily News* Sunday magazine. Kennedy mused that such ostentatiousness might be bad politics. Ed Plaut told him not to worry intimating that the ruled like to believe that their rulers lead more exciting lives. Kennedy said, "You may be right."

Regardless of whether Americans agreed or disagreed with Kennedy's politics, he remains today the most popular president of modern times. After the disastrous Bay of Pigs invasion, Kennedy commented to Arthur Schlesinger Jr. that he would have been thrown from office if he had been a British prime minister. Immediately following the invasion a Gallup Poll showed an unprecedented 82 percent approval rating. Kennedy remarked, "it's just like Eisenhower. The worse I do, the more popular I get. If I had gone further, they would have liked me even more." The below chart indicates that the Gallup Poll approval rating of Kennedy after two years in office remains today as the highest two year rating in recent history for any president, with Eisenhower a close second.

How Presidents Stood After 2 Years

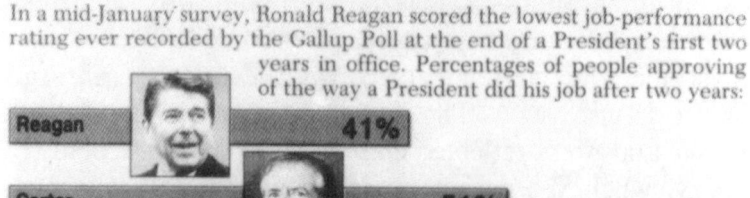

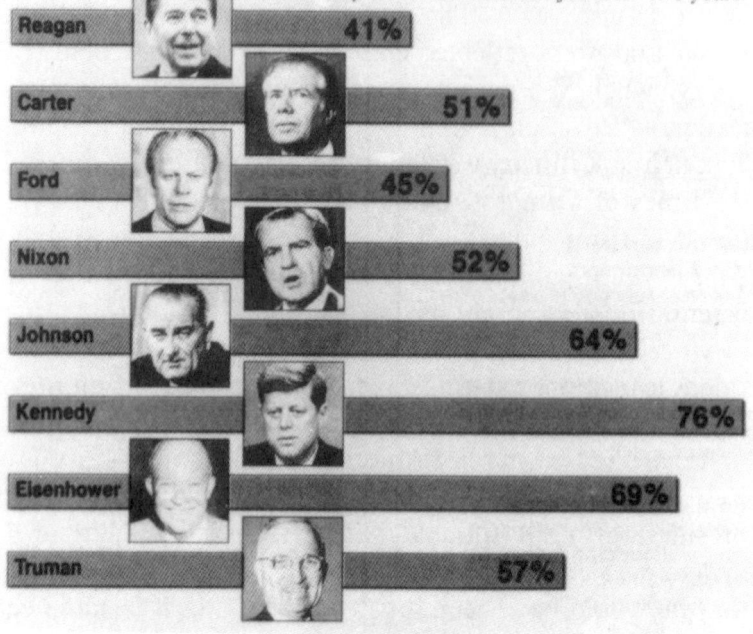

In a mid-January survey, Ronald Reagan scored the lowest job-performance rating ever recorded by the Gallup Poll at the end of a President's first two years in office. Percentages of people approving of the way a President did his job after two years:

Reagan	41%
Carter	51%
Ford	45%
Nixon	52%
Johnson	64%
Kennedy	76%
Eisenhower	69%
Truman	57%

As president, what kind of power did Kennedy hold over the press? Since he had befriended or impressed so many correspondents, Kennedy often had control over how reports were written. When William Manchester in 1960 was permitted a series of interviews with Kennedy for his book, *Portrait of a President*, he wrote Pierre Salinger, "I should be eager to have you review the facts in the completed articles." After the White House had reviewed his favorable account of the president, it was returned to the author without a word changed.

Kennedy, unlike Nixon, had a true interest and concern for the inner activities of the press people's world. As previously discussed, Nixon in the presidential race concentrated on wooing the owners of the press, TV, and radio stations, while Kennedy appealed to the working correspondents. Theodore White elaborated on Kennedy's approach to the media:

> Kennedy was interested in the politics of the media — its personalities, internal rivalries, best sellers, coming stars, fading giants, publisher's favorites, outcasts. He was interested in the newsmagazines like *Time* and *Newsweek*. Their internal politics of editor versus editor and putative replacements interested him as much as the politics, say, of Maryland and Delaware. On occasion, to a favorite of his, like Benjamin Bradlee, he would deliver an absolute scoop; or when William Lawrence later transferred from *The New York Times* to become Washington correspondent of ABC, he instructed Kenneth O'Donnell to give Lawrence, in his first competitive weeks, any possible break in the news he could. Kennedy enjoyed the thought that he could, by a word or a story, make a man's reputation.

Kennedy always appeared to be in control during live televised press conferences. Facts and statistics on various issues were always close at hand. Prior to every conference, he would study current issues and have his aides feed him potential questions. Occasionally, his press aides would plant questions. Mingling with reporters before a press conference, a press aide would tell a reporter, "You know, I think if you ask the president this question today, you might get an interesting answer."

During his political career, Kennedy always craved more and more television coverage. It gave him his best channel to the public. As president, however, he became outwardly concerned about overexposure. At the beginning of his administration he had Pierre Salinger count the number of fireside chats delivered by FDR because the public had found them so memorable. Learning that Roosevelt had only one or two a year, Kennedy decided to cut back on his TV appearances. Having used TV to win the presidency, Kennedy found that less coverage was better while in office. When asked by aide Arthur Schlesinger to utilize television more, Kennedy replied that he did not want to become the national bore.

At dinner one night, Kennedy raised the subject of news management with Benjamin Bradlee. He began, "You bastards are getting more information out of the White House — the kind of information you want when you want it — than ever before. Except for the Cuba thing, I challenge you to give me an example of our managing the news." Bradlee wisely did not suggest to the president that their close relationship could be construed as his managing the news. It was not uncommon for Kennedy to ask him what would be on the cover of *Newsweek* the following week. When informed that a cover story would be an anti-tobacco piece that would coincide with the surgeon general's report, Kennedy told Bradlee how sensitive this issue was to the White House since tobacco sales represented the economic lifeblood of many states which translated into national revenue. This was Kennedy's modus operandi for telling *Newsweek* not to be too critical of the tobacco industry.

Sometimes Kennedy would use the media to disparge certain individuals by suggesting that reporters look up their war records. Secure in his war hero status stemming from the PT-109 incident, he knew the war records of opponents would always pale in comparison to his. Bradlee mentioned one week the problems *Newsweek* was having getting Nelson

Rockefeller to agree to be interviewed for an upcoming story on him. Knowing that Rockefeller, a Republican, might become his opponent in the 1964 presidential race, Kennedy suggested that Bradlee look up his war record. Rockefeller saw no combat action in World War II since Franklin D. Roosevelt had appointed him to diplomatic service in Latin America. "Where was old Nels when you and I were dodging bullets in the Solomon Islands?" Kennedy asked. "How old was he? He must have been thirty-one or thirty-two. Why don't you look into that?"

When Edward Kennedy was involved in a senate race against Eddie McCormack, the president asked Bradlee, "When are you going to send one of your ace reporters to look into Eddie's record?" Kennedy then mentioned how McCormack had resigned from the Navy for questionable medical reasons on the day he graduated from Annapolis. "Dave Powers had all the information and he'll give it to you."

The wrath of Kennedy once focused on Arthur Krock, a *Time* magazine correspondent. Even though Krock had lobbied for Kennedy's Pulitzer Prize and worked loyally in the past for the ambassador, he made the mistake of not endorsing Kennedy in 1960. He refused to endorse Kennedy because he disagreed with the Democratic platform's stand on civil rights. The president encouraged Bradlee to criticize Krock in *Newsweek*. "Tuck it to Krock. Bust it off in old Arthur. He can't take it, and when you go after him he folds." Kennedy let Bradlee know of his disappointment when the articles were not harsh enough.

One virtue which the Kennedy's demanded from their friends was loyalty. Bradlee once made the mistake of making a presumed off-the-record remark about Kennedy's sensitivity to criticism, that found its way to print. In August 1962, *Look* magazine printed an article written by Fletcher

Knebel entitled "Kennedy vs. The Press." The subtitle read, "Never have so few bawled out so many so often for so little, as the Kennedys battle reporters." The following passage from the article got Bradlee banished from the White House activities for about three months:

> Even a good friend of the president, Benjamin C. Bradlee, Washington bureau chief of *Newsweek*, felt the presidential fire. Kennedy phoned him to take him to task for a *Newsweek* story about an old Massachusetts aide of Kennedy's being considered for a federal judgeship. Also ticked off later by Attorney General Kennedy for another story, Bradlee takes the rebukes philosophically and not too seriously. "It's almost impossible," he says, "to write a story they like. Even if a story is quite favorable to their side, they'll find one paragraph to quibble with."

One possibility that concerned Kennedy was the likelihood that servants at the White House might later write books or grant interviews about their experiences. The president had his attorney draft a statement wherein the undersigned would promise not to write about the Kennedys. Kennedy feared that trite accounts of his private adventures and family's personal moments would be published. When the press discovered that all servants were required to sign the statement, Kennedy had his chief usher accept responsibility for proposing the idea. He felt it would cause bad press to admit the control he held over his image.

The president's relationship with the media played a significant role in advancing his political career. Always the public relations man, Kennedy would publically smooth over his relationship with the media. At a televised press conference, he was asked to comment on how he, as president, viewed the press' treatment of his administration, and treatment of the issues of the day:

Well, I am reading more and enjoying it less — (Laughter) — and so on, but I have not complained nor do I plan to make any general complaints. I read and talk to myself about it, but I don't plan to issue any general statement on the press. I think they are doing their task, as a critical branch, the fourth estate. And I am attempting to do mine. And we are going to live together for a period, and then go our separate ways. (Laughter)

NOTES

139
"a rare quality or power": William Morris (ed.), *The American Dictionary of the English Language* (Boston: Houghton Mifflin Company, 1981), p. 227.

139
"You may be right": Ralph G. Martin, *A Hero For Our Time — An Intimate Story of the Kennedy Years* (New York: Macmillan Publishing Company, 1983), p. 231.

139
After the disastrous Bay of Pigs invasion: See Arthur M. Schlesinger Jr., *A Thousand Days* (New York: Fawcett Premier Books, 1965), p. 273.

139
"it's just like Eisenhower": Ibid.

140
How Presidents Stood After 2 Years: "How Presidents Stood After 2 Years," *U.S. News & World Report*, Vol. 94, No. 4, January 31, 1983, p. 7.

140
"I should be eager": Garry Wills, *The Kennedy Imprisonment* (Boston: Little, Brown and Company, 1981), p. 105.

141
"Kennedy was interested in the politics": Theodore H. White, *In Search Of History* (New York: Warner Books, 1978), pp. 466f.

141
"You know, I think": Martin, p. 308.

142
"You bastards are getting more information": Benjamin C. Bradlee, *Conversations With Kennedy* (New York: Pocket Books, 1976), p. 150.

142
It was not uncommon: Ibid., pp. 231f.

143
"Where was old Nels": Ibid., p. 76.

143
"When are you going to send": Ibid., p. 69.

143
"Tuck it to Krock": Wills, p. 87.

144
"Kennedy vs. The Press": Bradlee, pp. 21f.

144
"Even a good friend of the president": Ibid., p. 22.

144
One possibility that concerned Kennedy: See Wills, p. 111 and Martin, p. 316.

145
"Well, I am reading more": John F. Kennedy, *Public Papers of the Presidents of the United States (1962)* (Washington, D.C.: United States Government Printing Office, 1963), p. 376.

EPILOGUE

Media manipulation was one of the key factors in the political career of John F. Kennedy. His communication style also contributed to his success. Without television and without his special relationship with the press, Kennedy probably would never have become president. His mastery of the media helped him overcome an eighty-percent-Republican-controlled press. His political career demonstrated how the media can be employed effectively in the political arena.

By studying Kennedy's career, politicians will discover certain principles for handling the media. The prescription for media control follows:

- Acquire large amounts of money to purchase media time (TV commercials, political print advertisements, etc.)

- Befriend TV and press correspondents; treat them as colleagues

- Maintain a continuous dialogue with the media; praise it when it does well; point out its mistakes; be accessible always

- Create a politically sellable image; understand that image is just as important, if not more important, than one's stand on the issues

- Maintain a sense of humor when dealing with the media

- Develop a TV "presence"; remember the importance of physical appearance and proper grooming

- Determine the most appropriate medium and timing to convey a particular message

- Use public opinion polls to test political waters

By observing the above principles, politicians will have a starting point at which to begin when dealing with the media. Kennedy taught the lesson that a good relationship with the media can be a determining factor in winning a political race.

ABOUT THE AUTHOR

Joseph P. Berry Jr., a graduate of the State University of New York at Albany, holds a master's degree in communication from Fairfield University, Conn. He has served as communications director for Optometric Extension Program Foundation, communications coordinator for California Dental Association, as well as communications instructor at Junior College of Albany, N.Y. He currently holds a managerial position at Group Health, Inc., Albany, N.Y.